DATE DUE

FEB 14 '00			
JAN 16 2001			
MAR 15 2001			
OCT 26 2001			
NOV 06 2001			
MAY 10 2002			
DEC 10 2004			
OCT 05 2004			
FEB 28 2005			

FOLLETT

Hallucinogens

Paul R. Robbins, Ph.D.

—The Drug Library—

ENSLOW PUBLISHERS, INC.

44 Fadem Road	P.O. Box 38
Box 699	Aldershot
Springfield, N.J. 07081	Hants GU12 6BP
U.S.A.	U.K.

This book is dedicated to Bill Grant

Library of Congress Cataloging-In-Publication Data

Robbins, Paul R. (Paul Richard)
    Hallucinogens / Paul R. Robbins
        p. cm. — (The Drug library)
    Includes bibliographical references and index.
    Summary: Examines the history of the use of hallucinogenic,
or psychodelic, drugs, their physical and social effects, and the
dangers of taking these drugs.
        ISBN 0-89490-743-3
        1. Hallucinogenic drugs—Juvenile literature. 2. Hallucinogenic drugs—United
States—Juvenile literature. 3. Drug abuse—Juvenile literature. [1. Hallucinogenic drugs.
2. Drugs. 3. Drug abuse.]
    I. Title. II. Series
    HV5822.H25R63 1996
    362.29'4—dc20   95-39240
                                                                            CIP
                                                                             AC

Printed in the United States of America.

10 9 8 7 6 5 4 3 2

Photo Credits: Dave and Anne Robbins, p. 87; DEA, pp. 13, 15, 20, 22, 25, 36,
46, 50, 61, 65, 74, 78.

Cover Photo: "Images © 1995 Photo Disc, Inc."

Contents

Acknowledgments

The author would like to thank Sharon Hauge and Martha Weaver for their contributions to this book. He would also like to thank the Drug Enforcement Agency for the photographs used on pages 13, 15, 20, 22, 25, 36, 46, 50, 61, 65, 74, 78, and Dave and Anne Robbins for the photograph on page 87.

Grateful acknowledgment is made to the following publishers for permission to quote from their copyrighted materials: Bantam Doubleday Dell for H. Osmond "On Being Mad" in *Psychedelics: The Uses and Implications of Hallucinogenic Drugs* (eds.) B.S. Aaronson and H. Osmond, Anchor Books, 1970; Haight Asbury Publications for W. Andritsky, "Sociopsychotherapeutic Functions of Ayahuasca Healing in Amazonia," *Journal of Psychoactive Drugs*, January–March 1989; J. P. Tarcher for T. Leary, *Flashbacks: A Personal and Cultural History of an Era*, Grove/Atlantic, Inc., 1983 for M. A. Lee and B. Shlain, *Acid Dreams: The CIA, LSD, and the Sixties Rebellion*, 1985; The University of Oklahoma Press, for O. C. Stewart, *Peyote Religion: A History*, 1987; and HarperCollins Publishers, Inc., for A. Huxley, *The Doors of Perception and Heaven and Hell*, 1990.

The History of Hallucinogens

I looked into the glass of water. In its swirling depths was a vortex which went down into the center of the world and the heart of time. At one moment I would be a giant in a tiny cupboard and, the next, a dwarf in a huge hall. In spite of everything, I could, with an effort, behave almost normally.

—Dr. Humphrey Osmond, on using 400 mg. of mescaline.[1]

An equally strange and much more frightening experience was reported by a thirty-five-year-old man who was persuaded to use a drug known as DMT. Shortly after injecting DMT, he was swept into a world of terrorizing visions. He was wading into the ocean, where he was attacked by horrible monsters. Many years later he could still recall the feeling of slimy tentacles grabbing his legs, trying to pull him under.[2]

Mescaline and DMT, the drugs that brought on these strange sensations, are examples of hallucinogens. Hallucinogens are drugs that, in small doses, can produce changes in how you see things, think, and feel. These drugs can distort the way you view reality, and they can disorient your senses. Some users of hallucinogens may re-experience these effects at a later time when they are not using the drug. These re-experiences are called flashbacks.

Have you ever heard the term "psychedelic drugs?" The term psychedelic drugs means about the same thing as hallucinogenic drugs. Some writers simply prefer using one term to the other.[3]

The word "hallucinogens" may bring to mind the word "hallucination," which means hearing or seeing something that is not really there. The person hallucinating may be convinced that the experience (for example, voices he or she hears) is real. Usually, though not always, the user of hallucinogenic drugs realizes that the distortions in the way he or she sees things are the result of the drugs. True hallucinations, what occurs when a person believes that what is seen or heard is real, are one of the symptoms of psychoses, which are serious mental disorders in which there is often some loss of contact with reality. Patients with these disorders may hear voices or may imagine that people are plotting against them. Scientists have wondered how similar the reactions of hallucinogenic drug users are to the symptoms of these mentally ill patients. Some scientists believe that studying hallucinogens might shed some light on the nature of psychoses.

Some hallucinogens are made from certain plants. Eating these plants can produce hallucinogenic effects. Other hallucinogens are synthetic; they are made artificially by chemists in the laboratory.

Scientists have classified hallucinogens into different groups. One group of hallucinogens includes LSD, hallucinogenic mushrooms, sometimes called magic mushrooms, and preparations, such as yagé, which are made from plants found in South America and Africa. Perhaps the best known drug in the second group of hallucinogens is mescaline, which is made from the peyote plant. A third group of hallucinogens includes such drugs as Jimsonweed and PCP.[4] In addition to the drugs in these three groups, marijuana and hashish can at times produce mild hallucinogenic effects.

Hallucinogenic Plants

The history of the use of hallucinogenic plants is a long one, reaching back thousands of years. If we exclude the use of marijuana and hashish, the use of hallucinogenic plants in the old world does not seem to have been as widespread as it was in the Americas. One reason for this is that some of the best-known hallucinogenic plants are not native to much of the world.

One of the best-documented uses of a true hallucinogenic plant outside the Americas occurred in Western Africa, where *Tabernanthe Iboga*, a small bush with yellow flowers, grows. For well over a century, some Africans have made a preparation called iboga from this bush. In their book on mind-altering drugs, Andrew Weil and Winifred Rosen observed that some people who used iboga drank it as part of ceremonies that lasted throughout the night. The ceremonies, which included vigorous dancing, were followed by prolonged periods of wakefulness, then deep sleep.[5] Iboga surfaced in the mid–nineteenth century in Europe, where it was marketed as a tonic for all kinds of ills.

. Scattered around the globe there are peoples who, like the West African users of iboga, live in different ways than we are used to. Some of these peoples are nomads. They wander from

place to place, some with herds of cattle or other animals. Others survive by hunting, fishing, or gathering or growing food, often using simple, handmade tools. In their research, anthropologists (scientists who study human culture, customs, and traditions) have found interesting examples of hallucinogen use.

In the African nation of Mozambique, the Shangana Tsonga gave a hallucinogenic plant, *Datura fastuosa*, to girls entering adolescence as part of an initiation ceremony. The girls were told that they would see bluish-green colors under the influence of the plant, and indeed some girls reported that they saw green worms, snakes, and whirlpools.[6]

In Australia, there was a tradition among the native peoples of giving boys entering adolescence the pituri plant as part of initiation rites, ceremonies in which the young men were given the rights of adults in the society. Pituri produces hallucinatory experiences and illusions. Use of the drug was at one time widespread among the native peoples, but it stopped around 1950 when the pituri harvest was cut back.

The best historical evidence of long-standing use of hallucinogenic plants is in the Americas. While we cannot precisely date the time in which the native civilizations of Mexico and Central and South America began using these plants, we know it was many centuries ago. In Guatemala there are stone images of mushrooms, sculpted into the form of a god, that are said to be three thousand years old.[7] Mushrooms were used at a feast in 1502, the time of the Aztec ruler Montezuma.[8] In a Mexican medical library (Biblioteca Medicea Laurenziana), there is an Aztec drawing showing a man eating sacred mushrooms while a god with an unusual-looking head and clawed feet stands behind him.

8

Hallucinogenic Plants
and Religious Practices

It is important to note that hallucinogenic drug use among the native peoples of the Americas was often part of their religious traditions. One aspect of these religious traditions was an attempt to communicate with spirits for guidance and information. Often, the central figures in this effort were shamans, people who were considered to have extraordinary powers. It was believed that shamans not only could communicate with spirits, but also could predict the future and heal the sick. To draw on these powers, the shamans might try to enter a different psychological state. They might do this by putting themselves into a trance or by using hallucinogens. The use of hallucinogens by native peoples for this purpose is part of a long tradition that is practiced today in both North and South America.

In the upper Amazon area of Peru, Colombia, and Ecuador, the native peoples use *ayahuasca,* a brew that contains a number of mind-altering substances.[9] To make it, people cut down a certain vine, smash it with a stone, mix it in a cooking pot with another plant, and boil it with water for several hours. The resulting brew, which is consumed in healing sessions or during special ceremonies, is a powerful hallucinogen. Anthropologist Walter Andritzky tried it himself in 1985–1986 while living with the native people. When he used the drug, he saw "an immense number of very fast-moving figures, and later on quiet symbolic figures, such as an Indian standing on the moon shooting an arrow with a beautiful rainbow as his bow."[10]

In speaking of his hallucinogenic experiences, one of the healers told Andritzky, "You can travel wherever you want, visit your mother

9

or father, the spirit takes you everywhere, but other people can't see you."[11] After consuming a hallucinogenic brew, the healer talked about a vision of going to the mountains, where he encountered a jaguar that, in a goodwill gesture, gave the healer its fur.

Among Native Americans in the United States, one example of the use of hallucinogenic plants in religious practices is the use of peyote.[12] Another hallucinogenic plant used by some Native Americans is Jimsonweed (*Datura stramonium*). The Chumash people, who live near Santa Barbara, California, have used the plant. Jimsonweed has also found its way to the streets of America, where it is known by such names as Jamestown weed, locoweed, angel's trumpet, thornapple, devil weed, moon weed, and trumpet lily. Jimsonweed is a coarse weed that belongs to the nightshade family. It has poisonous oaklike leaves and lavender or white flowers. This plant may be found in roadside areas, and some people grow it in their gardens.

It should be stressed that Jimsonweed can be poisonous. The user may experience symptoms such as rapid pulse, dry mouth, flushing, and blurred vision. He or she may become irritable and confused and may experience both seizures and hallucinations. Some users have lapsed into a coma. There are reports that some Native Americans have died while using the drug.[13]

Synthetic Hallucinogens

Synthetic drugs—drugs made artificially in the laboratory—are an achievement of modern science. Synthetic drugs have proved very useful in the treatment of diseases. Some synthetic drugs, however, have hallucinogenic properties and have become abused on the street.

The best known of these synthetic hallucinogens is LSD. It is considered a semisynthetic drug; it was made from a natural substance—a fungus—but some laboratory chemistry was required to produce it. There are a number of less well-known, purely synthetic drugs that have hallucinogenic effects. These drugs are related to amphetamines and have very long chemical names. An example is 4-methyl-2, 5-dimethoxyamphetamine. Its short name is DOM. When DOM began to be sold on the streets, users renamed it STP. (STP is also the name of both a well-known motor oil additive and a rock band.) These initials of the drug were later said to stand for "Serenity, Tranquility, and Peace."[14]

The Drug Enforcement Administration (DEA) lists a number of other synthetic drugs that are classified as hallucinogens. The list includes 2, 5-DMA, PMA, MDA, MDMA, TMA, DOM, and DOB.[15] All the drugs on this list, which sounds like alphabet soup or a list of government agencies, are viewed by the DEA as unsafe and as having a high potential for abuse. Like LSD and mescaline, they are all illegal.

One of the more widely used of these illegal synthetic drugs is MDMA, which is sold on the street as "ecstasy." The drug was originally developed around the time of World War I as a weight-reducing drug, but it was never really used for this purpose. When the use of mind-altering drugs became popular in this country in the 1960s, ecstasy emerged on the streets of America. The use of ecstasy was particularly popular on college campuses: A 1987 study of Stanford University undergraduates indicated that nearly 40 percent of the students had tried the drug.[16]

Among the various illegal synthetic drugs, phencyclidine, or PCP, should also be mentioned. PCP is classified by the DEA

with the other hallucinogens, although some medical authorities view this drug as having so many bewildering, unpredictable, and varied effects that they classify it separately. The drug may act as an hallucinogen, stimulant, anesthetic, or depressant.

PCP originally was developed during the late 1950s as an anesthetic for use during surgery. Use of the drug for this purpose was stopped in 1962 because some patients experienced severe anxiety and delusions after the operation. For a while, the drug was used in veterinary medicine under the trade name Sernylan™, but in time the drug was discontinued altogether. In the late 1960s, PCP appeared on the street and was soon widely used. The drug often appeared in the form of angel dust: PCP sprinkled on mint leaves, parsley, oregano, or marijuana. Angel dust was smoked like a cigarette. Even in small doses (1 to 5 mg.) the effects of the drug are felt quickly, within a few minutes. The trip induced by PCP lasts up to eight hours.

The *Merck Manual of Diagnosis and Therapy* describes the PCP experience as one of "giddy euphoria," often followed by anxiety.[17] Higher doses of the drug (10 to 20 mg.) can bring on a catatonic state like that of some schizophrenic patients in mental hospitals; the patient appears to be rigid, in a stupor. Some of the descriptive terms for PCP experiences used by Ken Liska in his book on abused drugs include "agitation," "inability to speak," "eyes-open coma," and "zombie walking" (stumbling and crawling).[18] In its pamphlet "Drugs of Abuse," the DEA adds "numbness, slurred or blocked speech . . . a blank stare, rapid and involuntary eye movements . . . auditory hallucinations, image distortion as in a fun-house mirror, and severe mood disorders . . . producing in some acute

Phencyclidine (PCP) is an extremely unpredictable drug. In addition to performing as a hallucinogen, PCP can also act as a stimulant, anesthetic, or depressant.

anxiety and a feeling of impending doom, in others paranoia and violent hostility."[19] Sometimes this violent behavior is self directed, resulting in self mutilation.

In some people, the psychotic states induced by PCP have continued long after they stopped using the drug. Observers have noted that these psychoses are similar in many ways to acute schizophrenia. In both conditions, the person may find a sense of depersonalization (the usual sense of self, even of the body, is altered), thought disorders, and withdrawn dreamy states. In the 1950s, when researchers developed PCP, they thought that they had discovered a useful anesthetic. They could not have known that this drug would end up abused on the streets, sending thousands of young people to hospital emergency rooms.

The story of hallucinogens is both a very old and a very new story. It is old in the sense that some Native Americans have been using hallucinogenic plants for a very long time, and it is new in that even today chemists are developing synthetic drugs that have hallucinogenic properties. It is now possible for underground chemists to make new illegal drugs with hallucinogenic effects by slightly altering existing drugs. Ecstasy is an example of such a "designer drug."

Many hallucinogens have been recognized, and more are likely to be discovered. In an article on plants and mushrooms, David Spoerke and Alan Hall list more than two dozen plants that can be abused.[20] These range from familiar plants like nutmeg *(Myristica fragrans)* to khat *(Catha edulis)*, an evergreen shrub native to Africa.

When PCP was developed in laboratories like this one in the 1950s, researchers thought they had discovered an anesthetic. The researchers were unaware that their discovery would result in a street drug that would land thousands of young people in hospital emergency rooms.

Our coverage of hallucinogens will be selective. In the next chapters, we will focus on a few of the more important, widely used hallucinogens, presenting information about what these drugs are like and how they affect the user. We will look first at LSD, next at peyote with its major active agent mescaline, then at mushrooms, and finally, the quick-acting, short-duration hallucinogen called DMT.

Questions for Discussion

1. Hallucinogens can produce visual illusions. Visual illusions can also be produced without drugs. For example, if you sit in a train that is not moving and the train beside you starts to move, you may have the sensation that you are moving. Can you think of some other visual illusions?

2. Native Americans as well as other peoples have used hallucinogenic plants as part of religious practices. Why do you think the use of hallucinogens became associated with religious observances?

3. Hallucinogens often have a variety of street names. MDMA goes by the name of ecstasy, LSD by acid. Jimsonweed may be called angel's trumpet. Do you think these names make the drugs more enticing?

LSD

Lysergic acid diethylamide, or LSD, is probably the best-known hallucinogen used in the United States. It was discovered by Albert Hofmann, a researcher working for Sandoz Laboratories,™ a Swiss pharmaceutical company, shortly before the outbreak of World War II. Searching for new drug possibilities, Hofmann was experimenting with ergot, a fungus that grows on rye and on other grains. Using extracts from the fungus, Hofmann developed lysergic acid diethylamide. He was not trying to develop a hallucinogen and had no idea that he had done so.

Some years later, Hofmann experienced the powerful effects of this drug. He had been handling LSD in the laboratory without using gloves, and he did not know that some of the chemical had been absorbed into his system through his skin. Hofmann felt tired, left the laboratory, and began riding his bicycle. When he reached home, he lay down, lapsed into a

Albert Hofmann accidentally discovered lysergic acid diethylamide (LSD) in his laboratory shortly before World War II. Though the LSD Hofmann discovered was "semi-synthetic," most LSD found today is entirely synthetic.

dreamlike state, and began to experience a series of fantastic images—pictures with unusual shapes and intense colors.

Three days later, he intentionally took what we now know was a large dose (250 micrograms) of the drug to see what would happen. He again experienced vivid visual sensations as well as considerable anxiety, confirming what he had suspected, that he had discovered a powerful hallucinogen.

LSD has been described as a "semi-synthetic" drug. It can be made from the fungus Hofmann used, but it requires laboratory chemistry to do so. Most LSD sold on the street today is entirely synthetic. In their book on psychoactive drugs, Andrew Weil and Winifred Rosen observed that the nearest thing to LSD in nature is a chemical, lysergic acid amide, which is in the seeds of morning glories.[1] Weil and Rosen point out that not all seeds coming from morning glories are psychoactive. Among the morning glories that contain psychoactive seeds are Heavenly Blue, Pearly Gates, and particularly Hawaiian Baby Woodrose, a plant found on Hawaiian beaches. Since morning glory seeds are mildly toxic and can cause vomiting and nausea, it is no wonder that this natural relative of LSD has never been a popular hallucinogen.

When Albert Hofmann produced LSD in his experiments in 1938, he had no idea what he had discovered. When he finally realized what the drug could do, he must have had mixed feelings about it: The title he used for his book describing his discovery was *LSD: My Problem Child.*[2]

The Appearance of LSD

LSD is colorless and odorless. It has no taste. One of the important facts about LSD is that it has strong psychoactive effects in

21

LSD is sometimes placed on blotter paper such as the kind shown here. The paper is often decorated in bright colors, making it more appealing.

very small amounts, in quantities called micrograms. A microgram is one millionth of a gram. The amount of LSD sold in today's drug market is very small, but the drug can have powerful effects.

While LSD can be injected, it is usually taken by mouth. LSD has been sold on the street in many forms, in sugar cubes, capsules, or tablets. Sometimes, the drug is sold in the form of thin squares of gelatin, which are called window panes. Sometimes the drug is sprayed onto sheets of blotter paper and divided into decorated squares. Each square is supposed to contain one dose of the drug. The entire square of paper may be eaten whole. The names given to LSD on the street include acid, Green Dragon, Blue Heaven, sugar cubes, and White Lightning.

The Scientific Study of LSD

From the time of the early reports of the discovery of LSD, scientists were interested in studying its hallucinatory effects. A great deal of research was carried out on human subjects in the 1950s and early 1960s, when the drug was legal to produce and distribute. Researchers examined the effects of LSD on the speed with which people can react when they are given a signal like a buzzer. They have also studied the effects of LSD on a person's sense of how much time is passing and how well they perform tasks when under the influence of the drug. Some researchers have studied the behavior of people during psychotherapy. For example, researchers wanted to see what effects LSD might have on certain behavior during therapy sessions. They gave patients LSD before certain therapy sessions and not before others. All sessions were tape-recorded. Interestingly, the speech rhythms of the patients and the therapists, as indicated by such measures as

23

the length of time of phrases and pauses, became more similar to each other when the drug was used.[3]

In time, when it became clear that LSD was a very risky drug, government restrictions were imposed, and researchers shifted to the use of animals as subjects. Dogs, cats, rabbits, mice, rats, and pigeons all have been used in experiments. Some researchers were interested in studying how LSD affects an animal's ability to learn or perform. In one study, for example, researchers taught pigeons to recognize the difference between a short presentation of a stimulus (4.5 seconds) and a slightly longer one (5.5 seconds). They found that LSD decreased the pigeon's speed in recognizing this difference.[4]

The Effects of LSD

The National Institute of Drug Abuse (NIDA) describes the effects of LSD as "unpredictable."[5] One of the things that influences the user's response to the drug is the size of the dose. Larger doses are more likely to produce dramatic effects. NIDA reports that doses used in the 1960s and early 1970s were often in the 100 to 200 microgram range—at times even higher. Many users reported "bad trips" or "bummers"—frightening experiences.

Physical Effects of LSD

Shortly after taking the drug, the user of LSD will begin to experience its effects. Peak effects of the drug occur within thirty to ninety minutes of taking the drug. Among the physical effects that have been reported are increased heart rate and blood pressure, sweating, dry mouth, higher body temperature, dilated pupils, tremors, muscle weakness, flushed face, goose bumps, and chills. In its pamphlet "Tips for Teens About Hallucinogens," NIDA

24

These viles contain LSD confiscated from all over the United States by the Drug Enforcement Agency.

warns that LSD users run the risks of such toxic effects as convulsions, coma, and heart or lung failure.[6]

Psychological Effects of LSD

The psychological effects of the drug include visual distortions, changes in moods and emotions, panic reactions, flashbacks, and, in some individuals, psychoses.

LSD can cause hallucinatory experiences in any of the human senses, but the most typical experiences are visual. Colors seem to be brighter than normal, or they may appear to split up. Some people report seeing halo-like lights around objects, or seeing pulsating geometric shapes.

Can you imagine hearing colors and seeing sounds? While far from a typical reaction, some LSD users experience these strange sensations. The technical name for this crossover effect is synesthesia. A stimulus normally received by one sensory organ, such as the eye, the ear, or the taste buds, seems to appear in another sensory organ. NIDA observes that such changes can be frightening and may cause panic reactions.

Two of the frightening illusions that have been reported by a number of LSD users are: seeing Satan's face in space or on another person's body, and seeing friends' faces age dramatically while the user is looking at them.[7]

The sense of frightening unreality that LSD can produce at times is illustrated in a 1972 report by John Lilly, a well-known scientist. He had taken a large dose (300 micrograms) of LSD. He felt as if he was suddenly thrown into what he later called the "cosmic computer." He felt he was "merely a very small program in somebody else's huge computer." He noted that there were "tremendous energies in this computer. There were fantastic energy flows and information flows going through me. None of it made any sense." He felt total terror and panic.[8]

The user's sense of time may be distorted. A half hour may have passed, but the user may think that a much longer time has elapsed. Under the influence of the drug, some users may experience a sense that they can accomplish things better than usual. They may feel that they are experiencing unusual insights. Reality, however, may not back this up. LSD can decrease the ability to pay attention, concentrate, and remember.

Moods and Emotions

In the 1960s, when scientists were still using human subjects in LSD experiments, Martin Katz and his colleagues conducted a controlled study of the psychological state produced by the drug.[9] The study was carried out in a treatment center for criminal offenders. The subjects, all volunteers, were given one of four possible drugs. One of the drugs was actually a placebo; it came in capsule form like the others but was no more active than a sugar pill. The subjects did now know which of the four drugs they were getting. Some of the subjects received LSD. Testing of the subjects was then carried out at several times during the day with the aid of a questionnaire specially devised to measure the effects of the drug.

LSD users differed greatly in their response to the drug. Some people felt elated, though somewhat jittery. They seemed happy and giggly, with changeable moods. Other people became somewhat depressed. Their voices were sadder; they talked less, and more slowly. They felt tense and reported a loss of control. A third group of people reported experiencing conflicting emotions at the same time. They were the happiest

27

of the subjects, yet they were also the most jittery. They were both friendly and suspicious.

The researchers noted a striking tendency for very intense emotions to occur in some subjects without any apparent reason and without any accompanying thought process to explain the feelings. Examples were: "'I feel like I'm angry—I feel very angry—but I know that I have no reason to be, yet I'm getting angrier by the minute'; 'I feel like something funny has happened—everything seems funny, but I don't know why.'"

The researchers noted these effects brought on by LSD:

1. Very strong, opposing emotions may occur at about the same time. The emotions may not have a clear link to what a person is thinking.

2. A feeling of being out of control in regard to thoughts and emotions.

3. A feeling of being detached from the real world.

4. A sense of perceptual sharpness, but the perception of external things has an unreal quality.

5. A confusing perception of the world and of other people, who seem both friendly and suspicious.[10]

Anxiety and Panic Reactions

LSD experiences can be frightening. In a study carried out on one hundred LSD users in Toronto, 63 percent reported that they had at some time experienced a negative reaction to the drug. "The most common complaint was an overwhelming state of panic, sometimes involving terrifying hallucinations."[11]

LSD-induced terror and depression can last for hours. Users may experience the frightening feeling that they are no longer in control and are losing their minds. Feeling panicky and upset, a user may end up in an emergency room, accompanied by friends. They may have tried to reassure the user, to "talk the person down," but without success. Now they seek the security of the hospital to protect the user from harm. Statistics collected from a network of emergency rooms in American hospitals indicated that in 1993 there were more than three thousand episodes involving LSD. Many of the cases involved panic reactions.[12]

Seeking emergency help during a bad LSD trip can be important. Users may harm themselves or may become involved in a serious accident. In one study of adolescent LSD users, 20 percent reported that they or a close friend had been involved in an accident or had made a suicide attempt while using LSD.[13]

Flashbacks

A flashback is re-experiencing sensations that occurred with the use of a hallucinogen at some time after the effects of the drug have worn off. A flashback may occur months or even years after the use of the drug. While flashbacks have been reported with other hallucinogens, they have been associated mainly with LSD. Researchers studying flashbacks have reported that they can be nearly identical to the earlier hallucinatory experiences. The person once again experiences the effects of LSD he or she had experienced before, this time without using the drug.

Many LSD users experience flashbacks. While the estimates vary, in one survey of sixty-five LSD users, fifty described post-LSD reactions. In the years following the survey, 35 percent of the people continued to experience the flashbacks.[14]

Two case illustrations of flashbacks were reported by Mardi Horowitz.[15] The first case was of a seventeen-year-old male subject. He had been using LSD, DMT, and other drugs. During a recent drug-induced trip, he had had a terrifying hallucinatory experience of a dark scorpion on the back of his hand. The scorpion had many legs, and he was afraid it would sting him. The subject stopped using drugs but continued to see flashbacks of the scorpion. The second case was of a sixteen-year-old male subject who used both LSD and marijuana. On one occasion when he used LSD, he had a bad trip, with frightening images of a person being sucked into a whirlpool. A few weeks after the bad LSD trip, the image began to return throughout the day: On as many as ten occasions, vivid black-and-white images intruded into his thinking processes. Whenever the flashbacks occurred, he felt frightened and tried to stop them, but he was unable to control them. The flashbacks would stop eventually.

In addition to these dramatic re-creations of the LSD experience, some users reported seeing halos in rainbow colors around other people, and sensations that the sidewalk was bending, as if it were going downward. One user was left with a recurrent vision of a giant green iguana.

Researchers Henry Abraham and Andrew Aldridge noted that post-LSD-use reactions were sometimes brought on by such events as entering a dark environment, experiences involving feelings of anxiety, and the use of other drugs, such as marijuana. Abraham and Aldridge reported that some patients experienced post-LSD reactions for years and that the problem could be brought on by a single use of the drug. The fact that these reactions go beyond occasional flashbacks into lasting problems has led to the use of a new psychiatric term to describe them: "post-hallucinogen perceptual disorder."[16]

Psychotic Reactions

From the early 1960s, it was noted that some people who used LSD developed prolonged psychoses. "Psychosis" is a descriptive term used in psychiatry to describe a serious mental disturbance. The term is not usually applied to people who are experiencing problems with anxiety, phobias, or depression, but to those who experience breaks with reality. Symptoms of psychosis include delusions, beliefs in things that are not true (such as the belief that the sufferer is being persecuted), and hallucinations.

It is not clear just how large the risk is of developing a psychotic reaction following LSD use, but clearly there is some risk. In 1977, the cases of more than a hundred LSD users who had experienced severe reactions while taking the drug at rock concerts were examined, and 18 percent continued to show evidence of psychosis a year later.[17]

Abraham and Aldridge summarized some of the typical symptoms of LSD-induced psychosis. These are mood swings, mania (a state of hyperexcitement), visual hallucinations, and feelings of grandiosity (inflated self-importance).

It is not known whether LSD actually produces a psychotic reaction or whether the drug simply brings out psychotic tendencies that already were present in the user. The research data is still unclear on this point; it could well be that both cases are true. Nevertheless, it seems fair to conclude that LSD use poses a risk for the development of this serious mental illness.

Tolerance to LSD

Users of LSD rapidly develop a tolerance for the drug. This means that if a person uses the same dose of the drug repeatedly, the effects of the drug will lessen. The user may be tempted to increase the dose. That could be a serious mistake, however, because the negative effects of LSD are more likely to occur at higher doses.

A user who decides to discontinue LSD does not experience withdrawal symptoms; LSD is not a drug that creates physical dependence. LSD is not an addictive drug in the sense of producing compulsive drug-seeking behavior.[18] While not addictive, taking LSD can still be quite risky. We have seen how its use can bring on confusion and panic and how it poses a risk for the development of long-term psychoses.

LSD and the Brain

We know that LSD produces dramatic psychological effects, such as widely varying emotions and hallucinatory experiences. Scientists have wondered: Just how does LSD affect the brain to bring on such effects? Studies with animal subjects are beginning to reveal some of the answers. It has been found that LSD is a chemical that affects the receptors for serotonin, an important neurotransmitter in the brain. Neurotransmitters are chemicals that are involved in the transmission of nerve impulses. Serotonin plays an important role in regulating our moods. Decreased levels of serotonin are linked to feelings of depression in many people.

Rick Strassman reported an interesting case of a thirty-eight-year-old man who had been using LSD monthly. When the man developed symptoms of depression, his physician gave him a widely used antidepressant medication that also influences serotonin activity in the brain. When the patient started using the antidepressive, the dose of LSD he had been using was much less likely to give him a full hallucinogenic effect.[19]

Scientists are concerned with the possibility that LSD may produce lasting changes in the functioning of the central nervous system. One piece of evidence that has raised this concern comes from studies of visual impairment in long-term LSD users. Compared to nonusers, LSD users showed reduced sensitivity to light when their eyes had to adapt to the dark. The users' peripheral vision—everything they could see from the "corner of the eye"—seemed especially affected. The worrisome thing was that these impairments still were noticeable years after users stopped using the drug.[20]

Questions for Discussion

1. What would be the three or four things you would tell a friend who asked you about LSD?

2. What is your view about the ethics of studying the effects of LSD in experiments with human subjects? In your opinion, would it make any difference whether the subjects were people who had not used drugs but were volunteers or if they were previous LSD users?

3. What are some of the risks of a bad LSD trip?

3

Peyote and Mescaline

Think of a cactus plant. Do you see a plant with a cluster of spines, long roots, and perhaps flowers? The cactus is native to North and South America. There are around two thousand species of cacti. One cactus, *Lophophora williamsii*, is commonly called peyote. This cactus is hallucinogenic. Peyote is a gray-green plant. Unlike many cacti, peyote does not have spines. It grows in the wide valley of the Rio Grande in Mexico and southern Texas, under shrubs and in the open, and it has been found even in cracks on limestone cliffs.

While peyote is not a plant that is likely to attract a person's attention, eating certain parts of it causes a hallucinogenic experience. Peyote has a bitter, nauseating taste, and it often causes vomiting. The psychedelic effects of peyote come mainly from the tops of the plant. Hallucinogen users slice off the tops of peyote plants and dry them in the

This odd-looking plant is a peyote cactus. Although eating the tops of the plant—called "mescal buttons"—often causes vomiting, many people still use the plant for its hallucinogenic effects.

sun. These dried tops are called mescal buttons. Three to eight buttons can produce hallucinogenic effects.

The native people of Mexico discovered the hallucinogenic effects of peyote hundreds of years ago. Before the voyages of Columbus, the Aztecs used peyote for its hallucinogenic effects. Not long after the Spanish conquered the Aztec empire, a Franciscan missionary, Bernardino de Sahagún, wrote about the native people's use of peyote.[1] He related how it had effects like mushrooms . . . how the users saw things which frightened them or made them laugh, and how the people believed that it guarded them from all danger.

During the early days of Spanish rule in Mexico, the Catholic church tried to stamp out the use of peyote among the natives, even going so far as to include in a catechism, (questions and answers used in religious instruction) the question "Hast thou eaten the peyote?"[2] The practice was so widespread among the native population that despite inquisition hearings, the practice of using peyote continued throughout the period of Spanish rule and has continued until this day.

A 1902 account described a Mexican ceremony using peyote: "When the [peyote]-seekers arrive at their homes, the people turn out to welcome the plants with music, and a festival . . . On this occasion the Shaman wears necklaces made of the seeds of *Coix Lachryma-Jobi*" (a plant valued by the people). The night was passed in dancing. The Shaman then sang about how "he comes to cure and to guard the people and to grant a 'beautiful intoxication.'" Peyote in the form of a brownish liquor was served from a gourd, first to the

Shaman and his assistants and then, on some occasions, to the rest of the gathering.[3]

The belief in the supernatural power of the peyote plant spread to Native Americans in the United States, probably starting with the Caruizo and the Lipan Apache. Ritual use of peyote took hold in Oklahoma, and during the nineteenth and twentieth centuries it spread into much of the western United States and into Canada.

Peyote rituals differ somewhat from group to group and have changed over time. In *Peyote Religion*, anthropologist Omer Stewart described these rituals. The ceremony lasts throughout the night. The participants sit on the ground in a circle. There is a sacred fire and a sand altar. During the night, the participants sing, pray, beat drums, and eat peyote. Ceremonial fans and rattles are used during the singing. The prayers contain Christian elements; the name of Jesus may be mentioned often. It has been estimated that two hundred thousand Native Americans may use peyote in religious rituals.[4]

The Isolation of Mescaline

Peyote came to the attention of European and American scientists in the last years of the nineteenth century. After a visit to the United States, a German scientist, Lewis Lewin, returned to Berlin with a sample of peyote buttons and began to study their effects. In 1897, another German scientist, Arthur Heffter, discovered how to isolate mescaline, the major psychoactive ingredient in peyote. A student of Lewin carried out hundreds of trials of the drug on human subjects. He gave people the drug and noted the experiences they reported.

Mescaline Sold on the Street

When it is sold on the street, mescaline may come in the form of tablets that contain ground peyote or mescaline made in an underground laboratory. It is important to note that the "mescaline" sold in many urban drug markets is unlikely to be mescaline at all; rather, other substances such as PCP or LSD have been passed off as mescaline. A chemical analysis of samples of mescaline sold on the street revealed that fewer than 17 percent of the samples actually contained mescaline.[5] The uncertainty of buying a substance that cannot accurately be identified presents a clear hazard to would-be users.

The Effects of Mescaline

While the effects of mescaline are usually felt in about half an hour, they usually do not peak until about four hours after use. The effects of the drug may last as long as eight to fourteen hours.

Among the physical effects that have been reported after mescaline use are sweating, headaches, dizziness, dilated pupils, increases in heart rate and blood pressure, and a rise in body temperature. The psychological effects of the drug can sometimes be dramatic. The user may feel elated, may experience a sense of physical power, and may undergo hallucinatory experiences. These experiences are likely to be visual, though sensations involving sounds, taste, and smell do occur. Visual sensations that have been reported include vivid colors and geometric patterns. Some users have dreamlike sensations and become disoriented in terms of both time and space.

Firsthand Accounts of the Perceptual Effects of Peyote

In the late nineteenth century, German scientists were experimenting with peyote, reporting its hallucinatory effects. An American physician and novelist of that time, S. Weir Mitchell, also was interested in the drug. He reported on his own hallucinatory experiences from using the drug. His skill as a writer helped him describe the types of visions the drug may produce. In an article published in the British medical journal *Lancet,* he wrote the following about his experiences:

> *My first vivid show of mescal colour effects came quickly. I saw the stars, and then, of a sudden, here and there delicate floating films of colour—usually delightful neutral purples and pinks . . . then an abrupt rush of countless points of white light swept across the field of view, as if the unseen millions of the Milky Way were to flow a sparkling river before the eye. [Later the stars vanished and then] a white spear of grey stone grew up to huge height, and became a tall, richly finished Gothic tower . . . with many rather worn statues standing in the doorways or on stone brackets.*[6]

In his vision, Mitchell saw that the stones were hung with clusters of precious stones, some of which had the appearance of transparent fruit. They were colored red, purple, green, and orange. The purity and intensity of the colors were beyond anything he had ever seen.

In evaluating Mitchell's report, it is important to remember that he was not given peyote in a controlled study, which limits the scientific value of the report. In an ideal experiment, neither the observer nor the subject would know whether the subject had been given the drug or a similar tasting but inactive substance. Another firsthand account of the psychological effects of taking the drug was provided by the brilliant British novelist and essayist Aldous Huxley. On a May morning in 1953, he was given two-fifths of a gram of mescaline, and he noted his reactions:

> *Half an hour after swallowing the drug I became aware of a slow dance of golden lights. A little later there were sumptuous red surfaces swelling and expanding from bright nodes of energy that vibrated with a continuously changing, patterned life. . . . But at no time were there faces or forms of men or animals. I saw no landscapes . . . nothing remotely like a drama or a parable.*

Huxley began to notice that the flowers and books in the room began to glow with brighter colors. Red books seemed like rubies. An observer asked him about spatial relationships. Huxley noticed that the room looked rather odd, that the walls of the room no longer appeared to meet in right angles. He also reflected that space and distance ceased to be of real interest. He got up and walked about and could do so without difficulty. He had simply become indifferent to space.

When he was asked about time, he answered only, "There seems to be plenty of it." He had also become indifferent to time.[7]

Huxley observed that while mescaline intensified visual impressions, it left him with little motivation to do the usual things of interest in life.

41

Both Mitchell and Huxley reported the common reaction to hallucinogens of seeing colors intensified. Mitchell reported fantastic visions, while Huxley did not; Huxley lost track of time, which may happen with LSD use as well.

Experimental Studies of Mescaline

Like LSD, mescaline has been given to animals to observe its effects. In *Psychedelic Drugs Reconsidered*, Lester Grinspoon and James Bakalar summarize some of the findings: Under the influence of both LSD and mescaline, Siamese fighting fish move slowly, as if they were in a trance. Guppies swim until they hit the wall of the aquarium. When spiders are given mescaline, they weave irregular webs. Monkeys that have been given a variety of hallucinogens, including mescaline, show evidence of fear and disorientation under hallucinogens.[8]

A controlled study of the effects of mescaline on human subjects was carried out in 1992 by a team of researchers led by Leo Hermle working in Germany. The subjects were twelve volunteers, most of whom were physicians. Each of the subjects was given 0.5 gram of mescaline sulfate with some liquid and then was assessed for reactions within four hours after taking the drug. While the subjects were under the influence of the drug, their scores on psychiatric rating scales were elevated, suggesting that they were experiencing temporary psychological disturbances. The subjects' scores were especially high on a subscale called thought disorders, which suggests that their thinking processes were disrupted by the drug. There were also increases on scales dealing with such symptoms as delusions, anxiety, and depression.[9]

The researchers gave the subjects a test that is believed to be sensitive to brain functioning. In the test, two images were quickly flashed in front of the subjects. One image was that of a clearly defined face; the other image was that of a partially defined face, called a nonface. The subjects had to pick out the clearly defined face as fast as possible. Under the influence of mescaline, the test results suggested, there was a temporary decrease in the normal functioning of the right hemisphere of the brain.

Tolerance

Someone who uses mescaline often will quickly develop tolerance to the psychological effects of the drug. If the user stops using the drug for a short period of time, the drug will regain its effectiveness. There is, however, no evidence that mescaline produces physical dependence.

Views About Mescaline

Omer Stewart, a longtime observer of Native Americans' use of peyote, has reported relatively few harmful consequences for the Native American users. However, Hermle's study of the effects of mescaline shows that the drug can lead to temporary psychological disturbances. Other observers have reported that mescaline use has led to paranoia, fear, and suicidal ideas. Initial elation and laughter can give way to anxiety and depression. The probability of this happening is likely to increase with the purchase of mescaline sold on the street, because the chances are that the drug is not pure mescaline but contains PCP or LSD, which are powerful drugs with unpredictable effects.

Questions for Discussion

1. When the Spanish conquered the Aztec Empire of Mexico and began to rule the country, they tried to do away with the practice of using peyote. They were unsuccessful. Do you see any similarities between the difficulties encountered by the Spanish authorities and the current problems that drug enforcement authorities face in this country?

2. Mescaline sold on the street is unlikely to be pure mescaline. In fact, the odds are that it may be an entirely different drug. What hazards does this present to the user?

3. You may hear claims that peyote is a safe drug to use. How does the study by Hermle and his colleagues on mescaline bear on these claims?

4

Hallucinogenic Mushrooms and DMT

To many people, mushrooms are associated with a very tasty meal, adding flavor to stews, soups, and meat dishes. To botanists, chemists, and other scientists, mushrooms are an object of interesting study. Some scientists have been interested in the properties of mushrooms that might be useful in the development of medicines. There is, however, another side to mushrooms; some mushrooms have hallucinogenic effects.

There are many species of mushrooms. In *Psychedelic Drugs Reconsidered*, Lester Grinspoon and James Bakalar note that about ninety of these species contain psychoactive ingredients.[1] Some examples of the scientific names for these hallucinogenic mushrooms are *Psilocybe cubensis* and *Psilocybe semilanceata*. The popular name for psychoactive mushrooms is "magic mushrooms." The users of magic mushrooms have been called "shroomers."

The psychoactive ingredients in "magic mushrooms," psilocin and psilocybin, are in the group of hallucingens that includes LSD. A significant difference between magic mushrooms and LSD is that LSD must be created in a laboratory. Magic mushrooms are completely natural.

Hallucinogenic mushrooms grow in many parts of the world, including Southeast Asia, Central and South America, Mexico, the Gulf Coast of the United States, and the Pacific Northwest. The mind-altering mushrooms of the Pacific Northwest have been called liberty caps.

The psychoactive ingredients in magic mushrooms have the similar-sounding names of psilocin and psilocybin. Both substances are in the group of hallucinogens that includes LSD. Magic mushrooms can be eaten raw; they can be dried, stewed, or even put into a brew. Eating these mushrooms—particularly raw ones—may cause nausea and stomach cramps.

In his article on hallucinogens, Mark Werner notes that the effects of eating mushrooms begin within a half an hour after they are eaten.[2] The effects usually last less than four hours, but in some cases they could last longer. The hallucinatory experiences are usually visual, with distortions in how the user sees color. Werner notes that other effects of the drug include distortion of time and space, impaired judgment, and inappropriate laughter. Eating these mushrooms may bring on a number of physical symptoms as well, such as increased heart rate, facial flushing, dizziness, and compulsive muscular movements. As the intoxicating effects of the mushrooms wear off, the user may become drowsy and fall asleep.

Firsthand Accounts of the Effects of Eating Magic Mushrooms

The following accounts of the reactions to eating hallucinogenic mushrooms are taken from descriptions by R. Gordon Wasson and Timothy Leary. These accounts are personal reflections and are not scientific data obtained from disinterested users under controlled

47

conditions. In Leary's case, it should be emphasized that he was a leader in the movement promoting the use of hallucinogenic drugs.[3]

Wasson was a corporate executive, scholar, traveler, and adventurer who was fascinated by hallucinogenic mushrooms. Here is an excerpt from an article he published in *Life* magazine describing his reactions to tasting magic mushrooms in the highlands of Mexico:

> *The visions began with art motifs, angular such as might decorate carpets or textiles . . . They evolved into palaces with courts, arcades, gardens. . . . Later it was as though the walls of our house had dissolved, and my spirit had flown forth, and I was suspended in mid-air viewing landscapes of mountains, with camel caravans advancing slowly across the slopes, the mountains rising tier about tier to the very heavens . . .* [4]

Leary first ate magic mushrooms while vacationing with friends in Mexico. A professor at the University of Mexico put the mushrooms in two bowls on a table under a beach umbrella. Leary and his companions were told they could each take six.

Leary picked up a mushroom, and said it "stank of dampness." The taste was bitter. He had to wash it down. In a while he began to feel somewhat nauseous and detached; the feeling was strange, like going under dental gas. Then his thoughts made him laugh and he couldn't stop laughing. He got up and began to walk and his walk had changed to a "rubber-leg slither." He began to experience visual sensations, "Nile palaces, Hindu temples . . . woven silk gowns breathing color, mosaics

48

flaming with Muzo emeralds . . .: jeweled serpents." The effects lasted about five hours.[5]

Both Leary and Wasson reported that they experienced fanciful visions from eating the mushrooms. With visions of the beautiful, however, can come the ugly. Mushroom users sometimes become upset and panicky. In a study of adolescent drug users, Richard Schwartz and Deborah Smith reported that some frequent users of hallucinogenic mushrooms had accidents while consuming mushrooms, along with other drugs. There were incidents of head injuries from falling off roofs as well as incidents of loss of consciousness.[6] Mushroom users may also complain of exhaustion and depression. Like LSD users, mushroom users sometimes end up in emergency rooms. Flashbacks have also been reported with mushroom use.

Who Uses Mushrooms?

Eating magic mushrooms is not confined to the United States. There is a long history of use in Mexico and Central America. Mushroom use has also been reported in such countries as England, Denmark, and Thailand. Surveys of high school and college students in the United States indicate that usage is higher than one might suspect. In one study, usage among college students was 15 percent.[7] Analysis of hospital records indicates that males appear more likely to abuse this drug than females. Schwartz and Smith's adolescent drug users reported that the cost of magic mushrooms was relatively low—a dose cost seven to nine dollars.

Schwartz and Smith reported that the mushroom users in their study had trouble getting them. Mushrooms were not readily available. One of the sources for magic mushrooms was

49

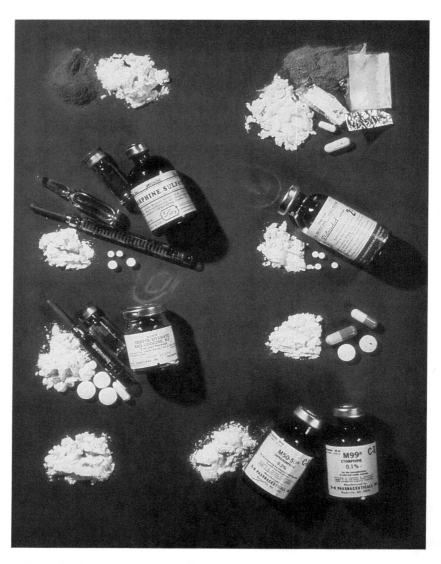

Although "magic mushrooms" are not shown among these drugs, experimenting with mushrooms can be extremely dangerous. It is very difficult to tell a magic mushroom apart from a poisonous one.

"home grown" mushrooms. Mushroom-growing kits have been advertised in drug-oriented magazines.

There should be a clear warning given about mushrooms. It takes an expert to distinguish magic mushrooms from mushrooms that are poisonous. People try unknown mushrooms at their own risk, and the results can be disastrous.

DMT

Weil and Rosen note that DMT is responsible for the hallucinogenic effects of some of the plants used by native South Americans.[8] DMT is unusual among hallucinogens in that it is ineffective if taken by mouth. The human body breaks down the drug before it enters the bloodstream. South Americans who use DMT turn the plant into a powder that they sniff. Richard Schultes, an authority on hallucinogenic plants, published a photograph of two native South Americans holding a long narrow tube. They blew the fine powder into each other's noses to produce hallucinogenic effects.[9]

Weil and Rosen describe synthetic DMT that is sold on the black market as a brown solid that smells like mothballs.[10] Users place small amounts of DMT on the tips of joints composed of marijuana, mint, or oregano, and smoke them.

One of the important things to know about DMT is that it is a very fast-acting drug. Users will feel the effect almost immediately, with the peak effect occurring very quickly. Users may be overwhelmed by visual hallucinatory experiences. Another unusual thing about DMT is its short-lasting effects. While some hallucinogens have effects that last for many hours, the effects of DMT can wear off in half an hour. As with other hallucinogens, there is a rapid tolerance to the effects of the drug.

51

There have been reports of people licking toads for hallucinogenic effects. Some of these reports are vague and should be treated with skepticism.[11] It is true that in southern Arizona there is a large toad known as the Sonoran Desert Toad, which produces a relative of DMT (5-MeO-DMT) in its venom glands. There are claims that some people have licked the toads for hallucinogenic effects.

DMT is also unusual in that it is made naturally within our bodies; it exists within our nervous systems. It is not known why the human body produces its own hallucinogen.

Among the scientists who have been studying DMT is Rick Strassman of New Mexico University's School of Medicine. He designed and carried out one of the few studies on the effects of hallucinogens, using human subjects, that have been carried out in the United States in recent years.[12] In Strassman's study, all of the volunteer subjects were experienced hallucinogen users recruited by word of mouth. Almost all of the subjects were men. On the night prior to testing, the subjects did not eat any food. In the morning they were ushered into a dimly lit room, where they were given DMT intravenously. The subjects were monitored for blood pressure and heart rate.

Some of the researchers' observations about the speed and duration of the effect of DMT were:

1. Subjects felt the onset of the effects of DMT within seconds after injection.

2. Peak hallucinogenic effects usually occurred before two minutes.

3. Subjects felt moderately intoxicated for another five to fifteen minutes. They felt relatively normal in about half an hour.

The drug was fairly well tolerated; there were no episodes of nausea or vomiting. At higher dose levels, there were increases in blood pressure, heart rate, and body temperature. There was also an increase in eye pupil size. At higher dose levels, all subjects "described an intense, rapidly developing rush that was both pleasurable and transiently anxiety-provoking, felt throughout the body and mind."[13] All subjects reported visual effects. These ranged "from intensely colored, rapidly moving, concrete, formed, more or less recognizable images with eyes open or closed, to abstract geometric patterns."[14] When the subjects' eyes were open, they saw geometric patterns with wavelike movements. The colors of objects seemed intense.[15] More than half of the subjects reported hearing sounds. These were typically high pitched, such as "whining, clattering, crinkling/crunching, or at times comical noises, such as 'boing' and 'sproing' sounds heard in cartoons."[16] As Strassman indicated, the effects of the drug included anxiety. Subjects reported a loss of control; they felt relatively helpless. These feelings usually lessened during the experiment. Some of the subjects reported that as they went through the experiment, their thoughts and their ability to evaluate what was happening were relatively unchanged. It seemed to some like a dream "in which, although awareness of the outside world was abolished, they were alert and attentive to the hallucinatory effects, remembering them quite well and in detail."[17]

Questions for Discussion

1. If someone were given supposedly "magic mushrooms" but were not certain they were the real thing, what would be the possible danger of eating them?

2. How does the idea of licking toads sound to you? What do you think might be the effect of the toad "venom" getting in your eyes?

3. How does DMT compare with other hallucinogens we have discussed in terms of quickness of effect and duration of effect?

5

Hallucinogens and Society

Hallucinogenic plants often have been used by native peoples in Africa, Australia, and the Americas for ceremonies or religious practices. Anthropologists have noted that this hallucinogen use is an accepted part of a cultural tradition; it is integrated into the ways of the society. People expect to see hallucinogens used in initiation rites and as an aid in healing.

This is not the case in our own society. There has never been a culturally approved tradition for the use of hallucinogens. Non-Native American society, as represented through its elected government and social institutions, sees drugs as an intrusion into the normal patterns of life—a cancer on the social body. The nation has made extensive efforts to reduce drug use. Congress has declared that our goal is to have a drug-free America.

To understand the beginning of large-scale use of hallucinogens in our society, one has to go back to the 1960s or

better to the 1950s, the post-World War II years. Europe was recovering from a devastating war. The United States stood alone among industrialized countries in having a thriving economy. Large numbers of veterans had taken advantage of the government's program for returning veterans, the G.I. Bill of Rights, which provided them with funds to attend colleges and universities. Millions of people were catching up for the lost time of the war years, marrying and raising families in a time of rising expectations. Divorce rates were low.

As the 1950s gave way to the 1960s, this relatively tranquil picture changed dramatically. The 1960s was a period of social change and social unrest. The civil rights movement captured the idealism and energy of young people to put an end to years of legal discrimination against African Americans. Anger and violence erupted in southern towns like Selma, Alabama. Overseas, the Vietnam War grew in intensity. In time, the nation became bitterly divided over the war. Some young people fought in the war; others joined the antiwar movement.

Many young people became disillusioned with what was happening in the nation. They decided to go their own way. A large number of young people rebelled against the values and traditions of society. They became part of what was called the counterculture. Labels such as "beatniks," "hippies," and "flower children" were used to describe them.

The counterculture stood for radical change. People in the movement wanted to end the war and to remake society. Many had "artsy" lifestyles; they read poetry, sang and composed folksongs, and dressed casually. Two outstanding symbols of the movement were long hair and the use of drugs. It is not clear why drug use became so tied in with the movement, but in *Acid Dreams,*

Martin Lee and Bruce Shlain viewed the initial surge of drug use as a protest against the establishment.[1] It was one way of saying no to authority.

In the mid-1960s, LSD use became widespread in and around college campuses. The Haight-Ashbury district of San Francisco became a center for hallucinogen use. Lee and Shlain described the area as the "world's original psychedelic supermarket."[2] One large-scale distributor manufactured LSD with a professional pill press, turning out pills with a dose of 250 micrograms each. These pills were sold or given away in large numbers.[3]

The Tale of Timothy Leary

Leaders often arise in social movements, helping to shape and push the movement forward. Probably the best-known leader of the psychedelic movement of the 1960s was Timothy Leary, a psychologist who was teaching at Harvard University. Leary became fascinated by hallucinogens. When he was introduced to magic mushrooms in Mexico, the experience changed his whole outlook on life.

When Leary returned to Harvard, he began to carry out research with psilocybin, one of the psychoactive ingredients in the mushrooms. In one study, he gave the drug to a group of students, most of whom reported that they had mystical experiences while under the influence of the drug. Leary later began using LSD at his home with his friends. His use of hallucinogens began to trouble some of his colleagues. Students on the campus began to use LSD. As Leary himself put it, "Some students quit school and pilgrimaged eastward to study yoga on

the banks of the Ganges."[4] Disapproving of his conduct, the Harvard administration fired Leary.

Leary's dismissal gave rise to publicity in national magazines. With a larger audience now paying attention, Leary began to support the use of LSD, talking particularly to young people. He preached a doctrine of "turn on, tune in, and drop out." Years later, having served a prison sentence for drug possession, when Leary was interviewed in *Psychology Today*, he stated that he maintained his interest in mind-altering drugs.[5]

The Siren Call: The Use of Hallucinogens by People in the Arts

Artists, writers, and musicians have always looked for new sources of inspiration for their art. Writers have sometimes turned to their dreams. Samuel Taylor Coleridge, for example, was said to have received inspiration for his fantastic poem "Kubla Khan" from a dream. In more recent times, some writers have turned to hallucinogens in an effort to attain visions and insights that would further their artistic expression. Aldous Huxley, author of the classic novel *Brave New World* and many other fine books, described his reactions to mescaline in *The Doors of Perception*.[6]

Lee and Shlain described a number of well-known writers, musicians, and others in the arts who have used hallucinogens. Most of the use took place when the drugs were still legal, and the users often took the drugs under medical supervision. Among the names mentioned by Lee and Shlain are Clare Boothe Luce, whose husband was president of the Time-Life Corporation; Ken Kesey, author of *One Flew Over the Cuckoo's Nest*; and Christopher Isherwood, the author of stories about pre-war

58

Berlin that were the basis of the Broadway plays *I Am a Camera* and *Cabaret*.[7] Poet Allen Ginsberg used hallucinogens and gave mushrooms both to other writers and to some friends who were legendary jazz musicians.

Does hallucinogen use actually improve creativity? There has been no convincing scientific research to prove or disprove this idea. Most of the evidence suggesting that LSD might enhance artistic creativity consists of self-reports from artists; these reports are interesting but are not considered hard scientific evidence. Stanley Krippner carried out a survey of 180 artists who had used psychedelic drugs. Most of them thought the drug had an impact on their work.[8] Some artists stated that their use of colors was bolder than before.

A few experiments have been carried out to see whether LSD actually influences creativity. A German researcher, Gerhard Grünholz, studied the effects of hypnosis and LSD on the work of visual artists.[9] He concluded that LSD added nothing to the work produced. With the current restrictions on hallucinogenic research, it may be some time before there is convincing data on this question. Meanwhile, the claims pro and con will continue to be made.

The Nation Reacts to Hallucinogen Abuse

Large numbers of young adults were using hallucinogens in the mid-1960s, and the doses were often high. The results included panic reactions, psychotic reactions, and trips to the emergency room. Stories of bizarre reactions to LSD began to appear in newspapers and magazines. *Life* magazine ran a cover story (March 1966) that was titled "LSD: The Exploding Threat of

the Mind Drug that Got Out of Control."[10] Public concern was stirred. Senate hearings were held. A series of laws was passed making the sale of LSD illegal.

Law Enforcement and Hallucinogens

In 1970, Congress passed a law, popularly known as the Controlled Substance Act. The law gives the Food and Drug Administration the task of evaluating the risks that a drug poses to the user, as well as the drug's potential for abuse. In making these evaluations, the FDA consults the scientific community and reviews the available research. If the FDA decides that a drug has a potential for abuse, the matter is turned over to the Drug Enforcement Agency (DEA), which then sets up the rules under which the drug can be used or whether it should be prohibited.

At the top of the DEA's list of controlled substances are Schedule I drugs. These are drugs that are believed to have a high potential for abuse, to have no accepted medical use, and to be unsafe.[11] Hallucinogens such as LSD, mescaline, peyote, magic mushrooms, and ecstasy all have been classified as Schedule I drugs.

There are heavy penalties for using and distributing Schedule I drugs. For instance, current federal law (21 USC, Section 841) states that the mandatory minimum sentence for possession of a gram of LSD (which would be considered evidence of drug trafficking) is at least five years in prison. A second offense doubles the sentence. A person caught with ten grams of LSD would get a minimum of ten years in prison. A second offense doubles the sentence. While simple possession of a small amount of LSD is considered a misdemeanor, a person could still get a

It is illegal to use controlled substances outside of the guidelines provided by the DEA. Using and distributing these drugs carry stiff penalties.

year in prison for a first offense, and two years for a second offense (21 USC, Section 844).

Controlling the Use of LSD

LSD, probably the most widely used hallucinogen in the United States, presents a difficult problem for law enforcement agencies. Because even a tiny amount of the drug is effective, LSD can be easily hidden.

Despite the difficulties, packages containing LSD are seized from time to time. The South Carolina Law Enforcement's Drug Analysis Department deals with about eight suspected LSD cases a month. In one case, a local police agency was informed that a package being mailed to a Columbia, South Carolina, residence contained LSD in liquid form. Law enforcement agents recovered seven plastic food coloring bottles, each containing an unidentified liquid. The Drug Analysis Department identified the substance, which indeed proved to be LSD.[12]

It can be a difficult task to detect LSD, particularly from urine and blood samples taken from suspected users. When consumed, LSD is almost totally changed by the body. The concentration of the drug in either blood plasma or urine falls to very small levels within a few hours. Detecting LSD requires very sensitive procedures. Researchers who have been working on the problem report that they have developed the means to detect LSD in tiny concentrations.[13]

Social Policy and Hallucinogen Use

People who support hallucinogen use have criticized the classification of these drugs in Schedule I. They have offered several arguments against this classification for hallucinogens: First, they have argued, hallucinogens are not addictive and are safe if taken under supervision. They are correct in saying that the drugs are not physically addictive, but their use is not risk free even under the best conditions. It is not accurate to call hallucinogens safe, because they can produce unpredictable reactions, sending people to emergency rooms in panic and distress.

A second argument is that some hallucinogens may have medical benefits and that not enough research has been done to either prove or disprove this possibility. A case in point is the drug MDMA (ecstasy). Some psychotherapists who work with people with emotional problems have argued that the use of MDMA might make progress in therapy easier. This question cannot be answered without considerable research, but there is a counterquestion: Is it desirable for psychotherapists to try to increase a client's openness by using hallucinogens? Many therapists would consider this unnecessary, and for many clients it may be counterproductive. The risk of increasing hallucinogen abuse could easily outweigh any benefits the drugs offer to the psychotherapy process—if there are indeed any at all. A third argument, which may have the most merit, is that controlled studies with hallucinogens may teach us more about the nature of psychoses. The argument is that this avenue of basic research into psychoses should not be cut off by unduly restrictive federal drug regulations. The studies of mescaline by Hermle and his colleagues in Germany, and of DMT by Strassman and his coworkers in New Mexico, point to the possibility that such research could be productive.[14]

Current Use of Hallucinogens in America

Since the 1960s, use of hallucinogens by Americans has continued, though not at the same level and without as much publicity. In National Household Surveys, which conducted interviews in a sample of American homes, people were asked about hallucinogen use. Three of the surveys (1991, 1992, and preliminary results for 1993) showed that about 8 percent of those interviewed reported that they had used hallucinogens at one time or another. In 1993, people in the eighteen to twenty-five-year-old and twenty-six to thirty-four-year-old age brackets reported the highest use, with figures of about 13 percent for the first group and 16 percent for the second.[15] When questions were asked about the use of three specific drugs: LSD, mescaline, and PCP, LSD was the drug most often reported, PCP was second, and mescaline was third. Other surveys suggest that hallucinogen use is higher among men than among women and more likely to occur in the metropolitan areas of the northeastern and western sections of the United States than in other parts of the country.

In 1994, about 11 percent of high school seniors reported that they had experimented with LSD.[16] These data indicate that for high school seniors, hallucinogen use is not typical; that is, most students do not use hallucinogens. Still, since about one in ten students has used hallucinogens, this translates into a large number of people, considering how many high school seniors are in the nation. It is clearly a significant public health problem.

In an article reviewing the research on LSD, Richard Schwartz noted that the drug is readily available. He observed that LSD is one of the least expensive, most long-lasting

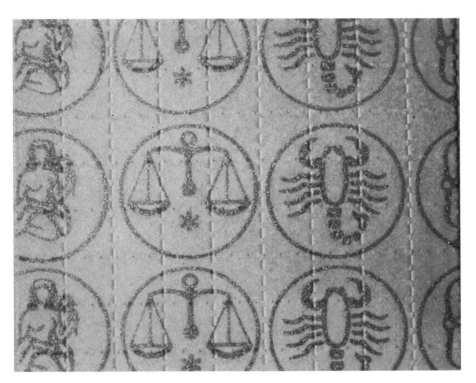

In a survey, out of three hallucinogens, LSD usage was the most-reported. Though there are many contributing factors to this statistic, its easy accessibility is a factor in LSD's high usage.

intoxicants that young people can buy. Schwartz called it "fifty cents per hour of high."[17] The low cost of LSD, as well as the difficulty in detecting it, probably have a lot to do with the drug's popularity over the years.

Native American Use of Peyote and the Law

This is a case of conflict between the state and religious expression. There are both federal and state laws prohibiting the distribution and use of hallucinogens. What happens when these laws run up against the constitutionally protected right of freedom of religion? The free exercise of religion is guaranteed in the Bill of Rights, in the First Amendment to the United States Constitution. For many years, Native Americans have been using peyote in their religious practices. Does the government have the right to force them to stop?

The conflict between federal and state government's responsibility to stop drug abuse and Native-American use of peyote in religious ceremonies goes back many years. Some states passed laws against peyote use long before the Controlled Substance Act of 1970. Indeed, many Native Americans have themselves strongly opposed the use of peyote. In 1940, the Navajo Tribal Council voted to forbid the use of peyote among tribe members.[18]

Many Native Americans have been arrested for peyote use. In some interesting trials, Native Americans were able to win their cases using, in part, a freedom of religion defense. In 1959, a Native-American woman, Mary Attakai, was charged with possession of peyote in Williams, Arizona.[19] She originally had called in the police herself, complaining about her brother, who

66

was drunk and disorderly in her home. Her brother turned the tables on her, informing the police that Attakai kept peyote in the house.

Mary Attakai was tried under a state law outlawing peyote. In the trial, she told about her belief that God had created peyote to assist her people in worship. The judge had to rule between the conflicting claims of the state and the Native Americans' right to exercise their religion freely. The judge ruled in favor of Native Americans. Here is an excerpt from his written opinion:

> *The peyote rite is one of prayer and quiet contemplation. The doctrine consists of belief in God, brother love, care of family and other worthy beliefs. The use and significance of peyote within the religious framework is complex. It is conceived of as a sacrament, a means of communicating with the Spirit of the Almighty—and as an object of worship, itself, as having been provided for the Indian by the Almighty.*[20]

The judge did not want the state to intrude into Native American religion. However, legal conflicts continued to arise, and the question finally reached the Supreme Court. The Court held that the First Amendment does not protect Native American practitioners who use peyote in religious ceremonies. Congress then stepped in, passing the American Indian Religious Freedom Act Amendments of 1994. This law stated that the use of peyote by Native Americans for traditional ceremonies was lawful and should not be prohibited by the United States or any states. The conflict ended with Congress deciding in favor of the Native Americans. For Native Americans, peyote in religious ceremonies was declared legal.

The CIA and Hallucinogen Use

In the 1950s, a government agency became involved in doing secret research with hallucinogens. This agency was the Central Intelligence Agency (CIA). The story of this research is found in Lee and Shlain's book *Acid Dreams*. Because the CIA as an intelligence agency operates under considerable secrecy, it is difficult for outsiders to be certain of the extent to which the agency engaged in this research. Nevertheless, Lee and Shlain provided considerable documentation for these charges. They related how some of these drug studies were carried out under the movie-spy-like code name MK-ULTRA.[21] The CIA became especially interested in LSD, looking at the possibility of using LSD as a "truth serum," a drug that could be given to enemy agents during questioning. To see whether the drug would work for this purpose, CIA scientists tested the effects of LSD on people in mock interrogation trials. For a while, it looked as if the drugs might be useful, but later it was realized that LSD was not a truth serum but a drug that produced many unpredictable reactions.

When the CIA began to experiment with LSD, some staffers began to worry about the possibility that the Soviet Union might also be experimenting with the drug. Some unlikely possibilities were imagined: What would happen if Soviet agents put LSD into the water supply of a battleship, or even a large city? Would everyone go crazy? Lee and Shlain described how the CIA contacted a Los Angeles psychiatrist who was working with LSD and asked him to calculate how much LSD would be necessary to contaminate the water supply of Los Angeles. The psychiatrist put some LSD into a glass of water and reported that the chlorine in the water neutralized the drug. He told his CIA contact not to worry.[22]

The CIA continued its experiment with LSD for a number of years. Lee and Shlain reported that among other things the agency wanted to find was what would happen to someone who was given LSD in a normal life setting without advanced warning. First, members of the CIA group studying the drug took LSD alone or in groups, noting each other's behavior. Then they began to slip LSD into each other's drinks. Once a CIA operative realized that he had been given the drug during his morning coffee break. Feeling out of control, he left the agency and fled across Washington "being stoned out of mind." He reported afterward "that every automobile that came by was a terrible monster with fantastic eyes, out to get him personally. Each time a car passed he would huddle down against a parapet [wall], terribly frightened. It was a real horror for him."[23]

In time, the CIA realized that experimenting with LSD was not useful for its purposes and discontinued its experiments. Public concern over what the agency was doing seems to have had a sobering effect on the agency. No more is heard about new CIA work on LSD.

Questions for Discussion

1. LSD is very easy to conceal and difficult to detect in users. If you were trying to reduce LSD use in this country, what strategies would you use?

2. The government and some Native Americans have had a conflict about the use of peyote in Native American religious practices. From the government's point of view, what would be good reasons to stop this practice? What would be the Native American point of view?

3. The DEA has listed the major hallucinogens as Schedule I drugs. This classification has restricted research on hallucinogens. What kind of research on hallucinogens, if any, do you think should be permitted? If there were research, what kind of safeguards would you insist upon?

6

Hallucinogens and the Individual

Why do people use hallucinogens? What are people like who use hallucinogens? What impact does the use of hallucinogens have on the life of the user? A study carried out by Reginald Smart and Dianne Jones in Toronto, Canada, helps shed useful light on these questions. The researchers interviewed and gave psychological tests to one hundred LSD users. The subjects averaged about twenty years of age and had been buying the drug on the illegal market. A few of the subjects had used LSD more than one hundred times.

The researchers asked what led the subjects to try LSD. The most frequent response was curiosity; about half of the subjects reported that as the reason. A smaller number, 15 percent, stated that they began to use LSD because their friends did. However, about half of the users received their first dose of LSD from friends. Peers can play a vital role in turning the idea of trying a drug into a reality.[1]

It is unusual for a person in our society to use LSD as a first drug; most hallucinogen users have already tried other drugs. Many use alcohol and marijuana before they decide to try hallucinogens. Many users of hallucinogens continue to use other drugs, in some instances, at the same time that they use hallucinogens. Questioning college freshmen, Christopher Martin and his colleagues found that some students use alcohol and hallucinogens at the same time. These researchers expressed concern that this practice might pose special risks because of the possible combined effects of these drugs.[2] The drugs could have similar effects on the user, producing greater negative reactions.

If curiosity and peer influence are motivations for trying hallucinogens, what makes people keep using them? Hallucinogens are not physically addictive; a person who stops using them does not become physically ill. The answer would seem to lie partly in the hallucinogenic experience itself. The vivid colors, the changing shapes, the visions that sometimes come, and the feelings that the user is profound and creative (whether or not this is true) can be intense. A person who finds life otherwise boring, or difficult and unhappy, may look forward to the hallucinogenic experience. A drug trip holds the lure of escape from reality.

The motivation to continue using hallucinogens has to be considerable because some trips are disasters. Smart and Jones reported that 63 percent of the people they studied had experienced negative reactions to LSD, including overwhelming states of panic.[3] It would seem that a traumatic experience like that would usually be enough to deter a person from repeating the act.

There is a push and pull of forces that hallucinogen users may experience—to use or not to use the drug. This approach-avoidance conflict is well expressed in a statement made by Oscar Janiger, a physician who practiced in Los Angeles. In the 1950s, he gave LSD to a number of people and tried it out on himself. He reported:

> *My first experience was in 1954 . . . It was not a uniformly beautiful experience. There were elements of it that were totally and remarkably transforming, and elements of nightmarish quality. So I got the whole treatment: the heaven and hell. There were parts . . . that were just so bad that I wanted out. And there were parts of it . . . that I never wanted out.*[4]

Personality and the Use of Hallucinogens

When standardized personality tests are given to a group of people who have had a history of using a variety of drugs, scientists are likely to find differences between the scores of the drug users and those of a comparison group of people who are not users. Smart and Jones found that this was the case for their sample of one hundred LSD users. They gave their subjects a well-known personality test called the Minnesota Multiphasic Personality Inventory (MMPI) and found that the LSD users scored higher on many scales indicating psychological problems.[5] Many of the users had conduct problems; they had difficulty conforming to the rules of society. Some typical examples of conduct problems are over-aggressiveness and anger. Other users showed indications of minor to major psychological disturbances.

Multiple-drug users tend to search for new and unusual experiences. Though crack (shown here) and hallucinogens produce very different effects, the reasons given for initial use of the drugs (for example, curiosity and peer influence) are often similar.

Smart and Jones's interviews with the LSD users confirmed what the test scores suggested. About half the subjects had been in treatment for psychological disturbances. They had been treated for anxiety, depression, behavioral disorders, and paranoia. Most of the psychiatric visits occurred before the subjects began using LSD.

Some of my own research with drug users involved experiments with tests measuring tensions relating to affection and autonomy (the need to be independent, to resist attempts by others to tell one what to do). Drug users tended to have more problems in these areas than nonusers did, and students whose drug use included LSD or mescaline were the most likely to have problems concerning closeness and independence.[6]

Multiple-drug users, which often includes those who have used hallucinogens, tend to score high on a test called sensation-seeking, which is a search for new and unusual experiences. This is a description that fits the hallucinogen user exactly. Hallucinogen use takes people out of the ordinary in dramatic and sometimes risky ways.

Finally, there is evidence of feelings of alienation, of being detached, separated, in the psychological makeup of some hallucinogen users. Smart and Jones reported that the LSD users they studied felt both "more socially alienated and self-alienated" than their control subjects.[7]

The Impact of Hallucinogens on Daily Life

The thing that prevents hallucinogens from presenting a daily risk to the user is tolerance to the drugs. A person who tries to use hallucinogens too often will get little effect from the drugs.

75

Use of these drugs has to be spaced at intervals for the drugs to have their hallucinatory effects.

Hallucinogen users seldom binge on their drugs. The huge expenses that come with some addictive drugs usually are not a problem for hallucinogen users. They do not usually experience the financial pressure that drives many drug users into crime to support their drug habit. Because of the tolerance effect, the place of hallucinogens in the lifestyle of many users is not constant. The problem, though, is that anytime hallucinogens are used, the trip can turn out to be a bummer, putting the user at serious risk. Hallucinogen use is a game of chance; the effects of the drugs are unpredictable. For a time, the user may experience few negative effects. Then disaster may strike, producing short-term nightmares and, in some cases, long-term problems.

The Family and Hallucinogen Use

In their study of LSD users, Smart and Jones observed that family problems were among the frequently stated reasons for users seeking psychiatric help. The researchers noted that the users' "family relationships were not harmonious."[8] Parents usually got their children into treatment. Another study carried out at about that same time by K. H. Blacker and his colleagues reported a similar picture. LSD users were described as angry both with their parents and at their own situation.[9]

In a study, Dusty Humes and Laura Humphrey carefully observed the behavior of parents toward their drug-using daughters. The daughters were polydrug users, that is, they had used a variety of psychoactive drugs. The behavior of the parents toward the daughters was described as "belittling and blaming."[10] The parents also seemed "conflicting and contradictory in their communications" to their daughters, showing both understanding and hostility.[11] The parents tended to blame the daughters for the troubles between them, rather than looking within themselves.

These studies should not lead to the conclusion that all hallucinogen use can be traced to difficult relationships between parents and children. There are many influences involved in shaping people's decisions to try these drugs. The personality of the user and the role of peers in providing the first opportunity for drug use are important. What the studies do suggest is that the role of the family is often important, and family involvement in the treatment program may be helpful in successfully resolving the problem.

It is one thing to say that the participation of the family can be important in many cases in helping the drug abuser stay off drugs. It is another thing to persuade some family members to participate fully in the therapy program; some members of the family may be unwilling. Daniel A. Santisteban and Jose Szapocznik, who are associated with the Spanish Family Guidance Center at the University of Miami, have observed considerable resistance among some family members to taking part in therapy for young substance abusers.[12] Sometimes a parent has not really been involved with his or her children. A father who has become distant from his family may be unwilling to become reinvolved in the therapist's office. Sometimes the problem is a family member who "protects the system," offering all kinds of plausible excuses why a particular family member is unable to attend. Finally, there are some family members who are afraid that during therapy sensitive issues may come out—issues that they prefer not to have surface. To expose these

The hallucinatory effects of drugs like LSD, PCP, and peyote may seem to take away the problems of everyday life, but these drugs can cause much bigger problems down the road. Arrests, fines, and jail time can all result from just one try. (*This photo is out-of-focus in order to protect the identities of the people in the photo.)

issues to outside scrutiny is too threatening, and they want to avoid taking this risk.

Herbert Waltzer's clinical report illustrates how LSD use can be a response to personal and family difficulties. The case study was about a seventeen-year-old who entered therapy because of his feelings of emptiness and depression. The patient had come from a middle-class family. His father had recurrent problems with depression and had been under long-term psychiatric care. The patient spoke little about his mother. He did not feel close to her. He told the therapist that he felt as if he had no parents.[13]

The patient had a good high-school record, and after graduation, he left home and went to college out of town. The transition proved difficult. He had trouble concentrating at college and soon became emotionally upset. Before long, he dropped out of school.

When he returned home, he found a job working as a clerk. He remained in poor shape emotionally, stating that he did not feel like a person, that he was in a trance-like state. He was fearful of people and said he had no identity or goals. He spent a great deal of time alone in his room.

It was at this point that he turned to drugs. In high school he had tried marijuana, but it had little effect on him. Now he tried LSD. The drug seemed to have a positive effect on him. He became less withdrawn and began to socialize with other people. However, the improvement was brief, and he returned to his disturbed state of mind between the times he used the drug.

He began to experience hallucinatory effects from the drug, seeing faces of people. These visions did not frighten him, however, and he continued to use LSD during the weeks he was in therapy. After several months, the patient dropped out of therapy.

It appears that this patient turned to LSD as a kind of self-medication to deal with his psychological difficulties. His earlier experiences, particularly those in his home, had left him unable to relate well to others or to cope with the stresses of life. Hallucinogens offered him a temporary escape from the unpleasant emotions that he was experiencing. Like many of the subjects in the study by Smart and Jones, this patient had both serious psychological difficulties and poor family relationships before he began experimenting with LSD.

Questions for Discussion

1. Research suggests that curiosity is the reason most often given for experimenting with LSD. Curiosity can be a compelling motive to try new things. What reasons not to try LSD would you offer to a friend who expressed curiosity about trying the drug?

2. In Smart and Jones's study, many of the LSD users were described as "socially alienated" and "self-alienated." Do you think such feelings of alienation: (a) led to the use of drugs? (b) were a consequence of a lifestyle of drug use? or (c) that both (a) and (b) are likely?

3. Sometimes family members are unwilling to participate in therapy for a drug-abusing adolescent. Do you think it is a good idea to put pressure on the parents to take part, or do you feel that an unwilling participant is more likely to do more harm than good?

7

How to Get Help

What should be done in an emergency, a severe reaction to the use of a hallucinogen? What is the treatment for a long-term psychosis following hallucinogen use? Where is there help for someone who wants to stop using hallucinogens and to begin living a life that is drug free?

The Emergency Situation

When hallucinogen users experience extreme agitation and panic, the situation may be a medical emergency, because it is possible that the user may do serious harm to himself or herself, and possibly to others. For coping with bad trips from LSD, friends may try to talk the user down. Talking down is a way of providing calm and steady reassurance that the hallucinatory

experiences that the drug user is having, and the troubling moods, are in fact drug-induced—the person is not losing his or her mind. Friends can stress that all of this is likely to fade in a few hours. In his article on hallucinogens, Mark Werner noted that while talking down is useful for LSD reactions, it is not helpful and should be avoided for PCP users.[1]

When talking down doesn't work, or is inappropriate, it is wise to go to a hospital emergency room. The hospital provides a secure environment. Here, the user may be watched for medical complications. It would be very helpful for the hospital staff to know what drug the user has taken, since treatments differ for different hallucinogens. For a severe reaction to LSD, some tranquilizing medications may be helpful, though support and reassurance are sometimes all that is needed.[2] In contrast, the treatment of a reaction to poison from Jimsonweed requires hospitalization and very careful monitoring. It is likely that the patient's stomach will have to be pumped.[3]

The emergency care for PCP intoxication can present special problems in that some patients may be unmanageable. A study of one thousand PCP admissions showed that more than one third of the patients showed violent behavior.[4] Such patients may have to be put in restraints.

As a general rule, the more information that can be made available to the hospital staff—including samples of the substance used—the easier it will be for the staff to decide on the proper treatment.

Enduring Psychotic Reactions

For users of hallucinogens who develop a lasting psychosis admission to a psychiatric hospital may be necessary. Here the patient is very likely to receive antipsychotic drugs. While a number of drugs (for example, Haloperidol) have been found to be useful, it should be stressed that not all patients have good recoveries from drug-related psychosis. In writing about people who have a history of hallucinogenic drug use and then develop a psychosis, Maryonda Scher and Vernon Neppé noted that some people face very difficult problems. They may have hallucinations as part of their daily experiences. They can become so distracted by these hallucinatory experiences that their daily lives become a shambles. They are unable to study, to concentrate on tasks, to work, or even to look at people when they are in conversation because of the visual distortions.[5]

Scher and Neppé described case studies of such badly disturbed patients. A twenty-nine-year-old woman entered the hospital complaining that she was experiencing both visual and auditory hallucinations.[6] The hallucination was a frightening one: People were trying to take over her body and kill her. In further interviews, it became clear that she was experiencing hallucinations in all of her five senses. The medical history-taking revealed that she had been using drugs and alcohol since she was a teenager. About two years before entering the hospital, she was using LSD heavily, as well as using alcohol and marijuana.

Treatment with antipsychotic drugs proved ineffective. She was then put on an anticonvulsive drug, Tegretol™. This drug seemed to help her, stopping some but not all of her hallucinations. When the woman left the hospital, she discounted the medication and started drinking again, and her hallucinations worsened.

Drug Treatment Programs

It is clear that hallucinogen use poses risks. Many people have experienced severe reactions to these drugs. There is an always-present possibility of disabling, long-term effects. As people become more aware of these risks, they may make a decision to stop using these drugs. It is one thing to think about stopping hallucinogens, however, and another to do it. Hallucinogens are seductive: Memories of visionary experiences can motivate people to use the drugs again. Making the decision to end drug use and holding to that decision often require help and support. A family physician or psychotherapist may be helpful. A drug treatment program may have the most experienced staff and may offer the widest range of services.

Drug treatment programs typically work with people who abuse a variety of drugs; the programs usually are not designed to work specifically with hallucinogen users. In choosing a program, a person should ask questions to satisfy himself or herself that the program is likely to be helpful in dealing with hallucinogen use. It is important to ask questions about the training and experience of the staff, particularly about their experience with hallucinogen users.

Research findings about the motivations for hallucinogen use suggest some additional guidelines for looking at the content of a treatment program. Peer pressure is a factor in steering people into using hallucinogens, so it may be useful if the program offers peer-pressure resistance training. This typically involves learning strategies of saying no and role-playing practice in doing so.

Because curiosity and sensation-seeking are elements in leading people to use hallucinogens, it may be helpful if the program offers assistance in finding new, more constructive ways

Treatment programs for hallucinogen users should encourage the users to find new, constructive ways to satisfy their need for sensation and excitement. Playing a sport like hockey is just one out of many rewarding activities into which users can redirect their energies.

to satisfy those needs. Introducing meaningful activities into the hallucinogen user's daily life may reduce the tendency to use drugs. Some possible challenging and rewarding activities that are available include athletics—running, skiing, mountain climbing—science, computers, political and religious activities, writing, painting, and music. There are many ways to enrich everyday experience, and a treatment program should encourage such activities.

Finally, studies suggest that the family life of the drug user has often played a role in the decision to use hallucinogens. When this is clearly the case, it would seem important that the family members become involved in the treatment program. This may not always be easy to do, and at times the conversations that take place in therapy may be far from pleasant. Still, for some hallucinogen users, family involvement in the treatment program may be important. A program that has therapists and counselors who have experience working with families can be a big plus.

The message that the use of hallucinogens such as LSD can be a risky business appears to be getting through. In a 1994 survey of high school seniors, students were asked for their ideas about LSD. When they were asked to evaluate the risk of taking LSD, 39 percent of the students thought that it would be a great risk to use the drug, even once or twice. Most of the students, 79 percent, said there would be a great risk in using it regularly. Finally, when the students were asked what they thought about people who used the drug regularly, more than 90 percent of the students expressed disapproval.[7]

Most students know that hallucinogens are risky, and most students don't use them. This is a wise policy. Not using hallucinogens is by far the best approach to dealing with the risk posed by these drugs.

Questions for Discussion

1. Are there drug treatment programs in your area? Telephone a program and ask what kinds of treatment they use for hallucinogen users.

2. Peer resistance training has been suggested as part of a drug treatment program. Drawing on your own experience, what techniques do you think work best for dealing with peer pressure?

3. Imagine that someone you know has taken PCP and has become violent. You are asked to help. What course of action would you follow?

Where to Go
for Help

The National Directory of Drug Treatment Programs gives addresses and telephone numbers on a state-by-state basis. If you are interested in obtaining a copy, try calling the toll-free number for the National Clearinghouse for Alcohol and Drug Information, 800-729-6686, to see if copies are available. The address of the National Clearinghouse is: P.O. Box 2345, Rockville, MD 20847-2345. Another toll-free number worth noting is 800-662-HELP. This is the number for the National Drug Information Treatment and Referral Hotline.

Finally, in each state and territory, there is a state office dealing with drug abuse. These offices may have additional referral information. Telephone numbers for these state offices can be found in the National Directory of Drug Treatment Programs.

Chapter Notes

Chapter 1

1. H. Osmond, "On Being Mad," in *Psychedelics: The Uses and Implications of Hallucinogenic Drugs*, ed. B. S. Aaronson and H. Osmond (Garden City, N.Y.: Anchor Books, 1970), pp. 26–27.

2. A. Weil and W. Rosen, *From Chocolate to Morphine: Everything You Need to Know About Mind-Altering Drugs* (Boston: Houghton Mifflin, 1993), p. 200.

3. For a short list of terms proposed as an alternative to hallucinogens, see S. Szára, "Are Hallucinogens Psychoheuristic?," in *Hallucinogens: An Update*, ed. G. C. Lin and R. A. Glennon. NIDA Research Monograph Series 146, 1994, p. 33.

4. The classification used in this book is based on that of M. J. Werner, "Hallucinogens," *Pediatrics in Review*, 14, December 1993, pp. 466–472. The scientific names of the three groups of hallucinogens described in this book are indole alkaloid derivatives, phenylethylamines, and piperidine derivatives.

5. Weil and Rosen, p. 101.

6. C. Grob and M. D. de Rios, "Adolescent Drug Use in Cross-Cultural Perspective," *Journal of Drug Issues*, 22, Winter 1992, pp. 121–138.

7. K. Liska, *The Pharmacist's Guide to the Most Misused and Abused Drugs in America* (New York: Collier Books, 1988), p. 180.

8. Ibid.

9. W. Andritzky, "Sociopsychotherapeutic Functions of Ayahusca Healing in Amazonia," *Journal of Psychoactive Drugs*, 21, January–March 1989, pp. 77–89.

10. Ibid., pp. 79–80.

11. Ibid., p. 80.

12. O. C. Stewart, *Peyote Religion: A History* (Norman, Okla.: University of Oklahoma Press, 1987).

13. Grob and de Rios, p. 128.

14. *"Drugs of Abuse,"* (Washington, D.C.: U.S. Government Printing Office, 1988), p. 49.

15. Ibid., p. 30.

16. S. Peroutka, "Incidence of Recreational Use of 3,4-Methylenedioxymethamphetamine (MDMA, 'Ecstasy') on an Undergraduate Campus," *New England Journal of Medicine*, 317, December 10, 1987, pp. 1542–1543. See also M. J. Cuomo, P. G. Dyment, and V. M. Gammino, "Increasing Use of Ecstasy on a College Campus," *Journal of American College Health*, 42, May 1994, pp. 271–274.

17. R. Berkow and A. J. Fletcher, eds., *The Merck Manual of Diagnosis and Therapy*, 15th edition (Rahway, N.J.: 1987), p. 1494.

18. Liska, pp. 206–207.

19. *"Drugs of Abuse,"* p. 50.

20. D. G. Spoerke and A. H. Hall, "Plants and Mushrooms of Abuse," *Emergency Medicine Clinics of North America*, 8, August 1990, pp. 579–595.

Chapter 2

1. A. Weil and W. Rosen, *From Chocolate to Morphine: Everything You Need to Know About Mind-Altering Drugs* (Boston: Houghton Mifflin, 1993), p. 97.

2. A. Hofmann, *LSD: My Problem Child* (Los Angeles: Tarcher, 1983).

3. M. Natale, C. C. Dahlberg, and J. Jaffe, "The Effect of Psychotomimetics on Therapist-Patient Matching of Speech Rhythms," *Journal of Communication Disorders*, 12, February 1979, pp. 45–52.

4. J. L. Altman, J. B. Appel, and W. T. McGowan, "Drugs and the Discrimination of Duration," *Psychopharmacology*, 60, January 31, 1979, pp. 183–188.

5. "LSD (Lysergic Acid Diethylamide)" *NIDA Capsules* (Rockville, Md.: NIDA, January 1995).

6. "*Tips for Teens About Hallucinogens, Quick Facts*" (Rockville, Md.: Substance Abuse and Mental Health Services Administration, undated).

7. J. B. Leikin et al. "Clinical Features and Management of Intoxication Due to Hallucinogenic Drugs," *Medical Toxicology and Adverse Drug Experience*, 4, September–October 1989, pp. 324–350.

8. J. C. Lilly, *The Center of the Cyclone* (New York: Julian Press, 1972), pp. 87–88.

9. M. M. Katz, I. E. Waskow, and J. Olsson, "Characterizing the Psychological State Produced by LSD," *Journal of Abnormal Psychology*, 73, February 1968, pp. 1–14.

10. Ibid.

11. R. G. Smart and D. Jones, "Illicit LSD Users: Their Personality Characteristics and Psychopathology," *Journal of Abnormal Psychology*, 75, June 1970, p. 288.

12. Preliminary estimates from the drug abuse warning network. Advanced report Number 8. (Rockville, Md.: Substance Abuse and Mental Health Services Administration, December 1994).

13. R. H. Schwartz, G. D. Comercí, J. E. Meeks, "LSD: Patterns of Use by Chemically Dependent Adolescents," *Journal of Pediatrics*, 111, December 1987, pp. 936–938.

14. H. D. Abraham and A. M. Aldridge, "Adverse Consequences of Lysergic Acid Diethylamide," *Addiction*, 88, October 1993, pp. 1327–1334.

15. M. J. Horowitz, "Flashbacks: Recurrent Intrusive Images After the Use of LSD," *American Journal of Psychiatry*, 126, October 1969, pp. 566–569.

16. H.D. Abraham and A.M. Aldridge, p. 1331.

17. W. Abruzzi, "Drug-Induced Psychosis," *International Journal of the Addictions*, 121, February 1977, pp. 183–193.

18. "*LSD (Lysergic Acid Diethylamide)*."

19. R. J. Strassman, "Human Hallucinogen Interactions with Drugs Affecting Serotonergic Neurotransmission," *Neuropsychopharmacology*, 7, November 1992, pp. 241–243.

20. H. D. Abraham and E. Wolf, "Visual Function in Past Users of LSD: Psychophysical Findings," *Journal of Abnormal Psychology*, 97, November 1988, pp. 443–447.

Chapter 3

1. O. C. Stewart, *Peyote Religion: A History* (Norman, Okla.: University of Oklahoma Press, 1987), pp. 18–19.

2. Ibid., p. 20.

3. Ibid., pp. 30–33.

4. Ibid., pp. 209, 327–330.

5. M. J. Werner, "Hallucinogens," *Pediatrics in Review*, 14, December 1993, pp. 466–472.

6. S. W. Mitchell, "The Effects of Anhalonium Lewinii (The Mescal Button)," *Lancet*, 2, 1896, pp. 1625–1628.

7. A. Huxley, *The Doors of Perception and Heaven and Hell* (New York: Harper Perennial, 1990), pp. 16, 21.

8. L. Grinspoon and J. B. Bakalar, *Psychedelic Drugs Reconsidered* (New York: Basic Books, 1979), p. 94.

9. L. Hermle et al., "Mescaline-Induced Psychopathological, Neuropsychological, and Neurometabolic Effects in Normal Subjects: Experimental Psychosis as a Tool for Psychiatric Research," *Biological Psychiatry*, 32, December 1992, pp. 976–991.

Chapter 4

1. L. Grinspoon and J. B. Bakalar, *Psychedelic Drugs Reconsidered* (New York: Basic Books, 1979), p. 17.

2. M. J. Werner, "Hallucinogens," *Pediatrics in Review*, 14 (December 1993), pp. 466–472.

3. T. Leary, *Flashbacks: A Personal and Cultural History of an Era* (Los Angeles: Tarcher, 1983).

4. R. G. Wasson, "Seeking the Magic Mushroom," *Life*, May 27, 1957.

5. Leary, p. 32.

6. R. H. Schwartz and D. E. Smith, "Hallucinogenic Mushrooms," *Clinical Pediatrics*, 27, February 1988, pp. 70–73.

7. Ibid., p. 70.

8. A. Weil and W. Rosen, *From Chocolate to Morphine: Everything You Need to Know About Mind-Altering Drugs* (Boston: Houghton Mifflin, 1993), p. 101.

9. A reproduction of the photograph is in Weil and Rosen, p. 102.

10. Weil and Rosen, p. 102.

11. T. Lyttle, "Misuse and Legend in the 'Toad Licking' Phenomenon," *International Journal of the Addictions*, 28, May 1993, pp. 521–538; R. Howard and H. Forestl, "Toad-Lickers Psychosis—A Warning," *British Journal of Psychiatry*, 157, November 1990, pp. 779–780.

12. R.J. Strassman, "Human Hallucinogenic Drug Research: Regulatory, Clinical and Scientific Issues," in *Hallucinogens: An Update*, eds. G. C. Lin and R. A. Glennon (Rockville, Md.: NIDA, 1994), pp. 92–123.

13. Ibid., p. 112.

14. Ibid.

15. Ibid.

16. Ibid.

17. Ibid.

Chapter 5

1. M. A. Lee and B. Shlain, *Acid Dreams: The CIA, LSD, and the Sixties Rebellion* (New York: Grove Press, 1985), p. 128.

2. Ibid., pp. 145–146.

3. Ibid., p. 147.

4. T. Leary, *Flashbacks: A Personal and Cultural History of an Era* (Los Angeles: Tarcher, 1983), p. 158.

5. B. Moseley, "Still Crazy After All These Years," *Psychology Today,* 28, January–February 1995, p. 30.

6. A. Huxley, *The Doors of Perception and Heaven and Hell* (New York: Harper Perennial, 1990).

7. Lee and Shlain, pp. 71, 120.

8. S. Krippner, "The Influence of 'Psychedelic' Experience on Contemporary Art and Music," in *Hallucinogenic Drug Research: Impact on Science and Society,* ed. J. R. Gamage and E. L. Zerkin (Beloit, Wis.: Stash Press, 1997), pp. 83–114.

9. G. Grünholz, "From LSD to Self-Hypnosis in Catathymic Experience, Art and Therapy," *Zeitschrift für Psychotherapie und Medizinische Psychologie,* 21, March 1971, pp. 74–86.

10. Lee and Shlain, p. 150.

11. For a description of the government's regulatory process, see R. S. Gable, "Regulatory Risk Management of Psychoactive Substances," *Law and Policy,* 14 October 1992, p. 262.

12. S.D. Kilmer, "The Isolation and Identification of Lysergic Acid Diethylamide (LSD) from Sugar Cubes and a Liquid Substrate," *Journal of Forensic Sciences,* 39, May 1994, pp. 860–862.

13. C.C. Nelson and R.L. Foltz, "Chromatographic and Mass Spectrometric Methods for Determination of Lysergic Acid Diethylamide (LSD) and Metabolites in Body Fluids," *Journal of Chromatography,* 580, September 1992, pp. 97–109.

14. L. Hermle et al., "Mescaline-induced Psychopathological, Neuropsychological, and Neurometabolic Effects in Normal Subjects: Experimental Psychosis as a Tool for Psychiatric Research," *Biological Psychiatry*, 32, December 1992, pp. 976–981; R. J. Strassman, "Human Hallucinogenic Drug Research: Regulatory, Clinical and Scientific Issues," in *Hallucinogens, An Update* ed. G. C. Lin and R. A. Glennon (Rockville, Md.: NIDA), pp. 92–123.

15. Preliminary estimates from the 1993 National Household Survey on Drug Abuse: Advanced Report Number 7. (Rockville, Md.: Substance Abuse and Mental Health Administration, July 1994), pp. 49, 53, 55.

16. *"LSD (Lysergic Acid Diethylamide),"* NIDA Capsules Rockville, Md.: NIDA, January 1995.

17. R. H. Schwartz, "LSD: Its Rise, Fall, and Renewed Popularity Among High School Students," *Pediatric Clinics of North America*. In press.

18. O.C. Stewart, *Peyote Religion: A History* (Norman, Okla.: University of Oklahoma Press, 1987), p. 296.

19. Ibid., p. 305.

20. Ibid., p. 307.

21. Lee and Shlain, p. 28.

22. Ibid., p. 21.

23. Ibid., p. 30.

Chapter 6

1. R. G. Smart and D. Jones, "Illicit LSD Users: Their Personality Characteristics and Psychopathology," *Journal of Abnormal Psychology*, 75, June 1970, pp. 286–292.

2. C.S. Martin, P.R. Clifford, and R.L. Clapper, "Patterns and Predictors of Simultaneous and Concurrent Use of Alcohol, Tobacco, Marijuana, and Hallucinogens in First-Year College Students," *Journal of Substance Abuse*, 4, 1992, pp. 319–326.

3. Smart and Jones, pp. 288–289.

4. T. Leary, *Flashbacks: A Personal and Cultural History of an Era* (Los Angeles: Tarcher, 1983), p. 132.

5. Smart and Jones, pp. 288–289.

6. P.R. Robbins, R. H. Tanck, and H.A. Meyersburg, "Psychological Factors in Smoking, Drinking, and Drug Experimentation," *Journal of Clinical Psychology*, 27, October 1971, pp. 450–452.

7. Smart and Jones, p. 291.

8. Ibid., p. 290.

9. K.H. Blacker et al., "Chronic Users of LSD: 'The Acid-heads,'" *American Journal of Psychiatry*, 125, September 1968, pp. 97–107.

10. D.L. Humes and L.L. Humphrey, "A Multimethod Analysis of Families with a Polydrug-Dependent or Normal Adolescent Daughter," *Journal of Abnormal Psychology*, 103, November 1994, pp. 676–685.

11. Ibid., p. 682.

12. D.A. Santisteban and J. Szapocznik, "Bridging Theory, Research, and Practice to More Successfully Engage Substance Abusing Youth and Their Families into Therapy," *Journal of Child and Adolescent Substance Abuse*, 3, 1994, pp. 9–24.

13. H. Waltzer, "Depersonalization and the Use of LSD: A Psychodynamic Study," *American Journal of Psychoanalysis*, 32, May 1972, pp. 45–52.

Chapter 7

1. M.J. Werner, "Hallucinogens," *Pediatrics in Review*, 14, December 1993, pp. 466–472.

2. J.B. Leikin et al., "Clinical Features and Management of Intoxication Due to Hallucinogenic Drugs," *Medical Toxicology and Adverse Drug Experience*, 4, September–October 1989, pp. 324–350, 343.

3. Ibid., p. 344.

4. Ibid., p. 332.

5. M. Scher and V. Neppé, "Carbamazepine Adjunct for Nonresponsive Psychosis with Prior Hallucinogenic Abuse," *Journal of Nervous and Mental Disease*, 177, December 1989, pp. 755–757.

6. Ibid., p. 756.

7. "*LSD (Lysergic Acid Diethylamide)*," *NIDA Capsules*, (Rockville, Md.: NIDA, January 1995.)

Glossary

antipsychotic drug—A drug used to treat psychoses.

catatonic—A marked psychological disturbance in which the person may be in a stupor. He or she may be mute.

DMT—A hallucinogen that is made in the brain. It is also found in plants used by Native Americans in South America and has been synthesized.

DOM—Also known as STP; a synthetic hallucinogen chemically related to amphetamines.

ecstasy—A street name for the synthetic drug 3,4-methylenedioxymethamphetamine (MDMA). It has both stimulant and hallucinogenic properties.

flashback—A recurrence of a drug-induced hallucinatory experience some time after the drug has been taken.

hallucination—Perception of something that is not actually there. This may be seeing something that no one else can see or hearing voices that no one else hears.

hallucinogen—A drug that if taken in small doses produces changes in perception, thought, and mood.

iboga—A brew made from a plant growing in Africa that has hallucinogenic and stimulant properties.

indole alkaloid derivatives—A group of hallucinogens. LSD is the best-known drug in this group.

Jimsonweed—A member of the nightshade family. Eating the seeds of this plant can produce hallucinogenic effects.

LSD (lysergic acid diethylamide)—A powerful hallucinogen discovered by experiments with the ergot fungus. It is now usually synthesized.

magic mushrooms—Certain mushrooms that produce hallucinogenic effects.

mescal buttons—The tops of the peyote plant that are cut off, often sun-dried, and then eaten for hallucinogenic effects.

mescaline—The psychoactive ingredient in the peyote plant.

microgram—One millionth of a gram.

panic reaction—A reaction characterized by intense anxiety that may include physical symptoms such as faintness, shaking, and smothering sensations. The person may have fears of losing his or her mind and dying. This is a fairly common disorder that can happen to many people who do not use drugs.

PCP (phencyclidine)—Known on the street under many names, such as Angel Dust, Supergrass, and Rocket Fuel. Its effects are varied and unpredictable.

peyote—A hallucinogenic cactus found in parts of Mexico and Texas. It is widely used among Native Americans in religious ceremonies.

phenylethylamines—A group of hallucinogenic drugs. Probably the best known of these is mescaline.

piperidine derivatives—A group of hallucinogens of which the best known are PCP and Jimsonweed.

post-hallucinogen perceptual disorder—A term similar to "flashback." It refers to the recurrence of drug-induced hallucinatory states at some time after use of the drug is stopped.

psilocin—A psychoactive ingredient found in magic mushrooms. Like psilocybin, it is an indole alkaloid hallucinogen.

psilocybin—A psychoactive ingredient found in magic mushrooms.

psychoactive—Altering one's thinking, perceptions, and emotions. Drugs that do this are called psychoactive drugs.

psychosis—A mental disorder in which there is often some loss of reality contact. Symptoms can include delusions and hallucinations.

serotonin—One of the chemicals that plays an important role in the transmission of messages within the brain and through the nervous system. Such chemicals are called neurotransmitters.

shaman—A person who acts as a communicator between the everyday world and the supernatural, using his or her perceived powers to cure illness and to predict the future.

synesthesia—Distorted perceptions in which sensations appear to cross over from the usual sensory receptor to another. The person may experience the sensation of hearing colors or seeing sounds.

tolerance—Reduction of the response to a drug following its repeated use.

Bibliography

Abraham, Henry D., and Andrew M. Aldridge. "Adverse Consequences of Lysergic Acid Diethylamide." *Addiction*, 88 (October 1993).

Abraham, Henry D., and Ernst Wolf. "Visual Function in Past Users of LSD: Psychophysical Findings." *Journal of Abnormal Psychology*, 97 (November 1988).

Abruzzi, W. "Drug-induced Psychosis." *International Journal of the Addictions*, 121 (1977).

Altman, Jack L., James B. Appel, and William T. McGowan. "Drugs and the Discrimination of Duration." *Psychopharmacology*, 60 (1979).

Andritzky, Walter. "Sociopsychotherapeutic Functions of Ayahuasca Healing in Amazonia." *Journal of Psychoactive Drugs*, 21 (January–March 1989).

Berkow, Robert, and Andrew J. Fletcher (eds.). *The Merck Manual of Diagnosis and Therapy, 15th edition.* Rahway, N.J.: Merck, Sharpe and Dohme Research Laboratories, 1987.

Blacker, K. H., et al. "Chronic Users of LSD: The 'Acidheads'." *American Journal of Psychiatry*, 125 (September 1968).

Cuomo, M. J., P. G. Dyment, and V. M. Gammino. "Increasing Use of Ecstasy (MDMA) and Other Hallucinogens on a College Campus." *Journal of American College Health*, 42 (May 1994).

"*Drugs of Abuse.*" First published as Volume 6, No. 2 of *Drug Enforcement Magazine*, 1975. Available from Washington, D.C.: U.S. Government Printing Office.

Gable, Robert S. "Regulatory Risk Management of Psychoactive Substances." *Law and Policy*, 14 (October 1992).

Grinspoon, Lester, and James B. Bakalar. *Psychedelic Drugs Reconsidered.* New York: Basic Books, 1979.

Grob, Charles, and Marlene D. de Rios. "Adolescent Drug Use in Cross-Cultural Perspective." *Journal of Drug Issues,* 22 (Winter 1992).

Grünholz, Gerhard. "From LSD to Self-Hypnosis in Catathymic Experience, Art and Therapy." *Zeitschrift für Psychotherapie und Medizinische Psychologie,* 21 (March 1971).

Hermle, Leo, et al. "Mescaline-Induced Psychopathological, Neuropsychological, and Neurometabolic Effects in Normal Subjects: Experimental Psychosis as a Tool for Psychiatric Research." *Biological Psychiatry,* 32 (December 1992).

Hofmann, Albert. *LSD: My Problem Child.* Los Angeles: Tarcher, 1983.

Horowitz, Mardi J. "Flashbacks: Recurrent Intrusive Images After the Use of LSD." *American Journal of Psychiatry,* 126 (October 1969).

Howard, R., and H. Forestl, "Toad-Lickers Psychosis—A Warning." *British Journal of Psychiatry,* 157 (November 9, 1990).

Humes, Dusty L., and Laura L. Humphrey. "A Multimethod Analysis of Families with a Polydrug-Dependent or Normal Adolescent Daughter." *Journal of Abnormal Psychology,* 103 (November 1994).

Huxley, Aldous. *The Doors of Perception and Heaven and Hell.* New York: Harper Perennial, 1990.

Katz, Martin M., Irene E. Waskow, and James Olsson. "Characterizing the Psychological State Produced by LSD." *Journal of Abnormal Psychology,* 73 (February 1968).

Kilmer, Susan D. "The Isolation and Identification of Lysergic Acid Diethylamide (LSD) from Sugar Cubes and a Liquid Substrate." *Journal of Forensic Sciences,* (May 1994).

Krippner, Stanley. "The Influence of 'Psychedelic' Experience on Contemporary Art and Music," in James R. Gamage and Edmund L. Zerkin (eds.), *Hallucinogenic Drug Research: Impact on Science and Society.* Beloit, Wis.: Stash Press, 1970.

Leary, Timothy. *Flashbacks: A Personal and Cultural History of an Era.* Los Angeles: Tarcher, 1983.

Lee, Martin A., and Bruce Shlain. *Acid Dreams: The CIA, LSD, and the Sixties Rebellion*. New York: Grove Press, 1985.

Leikin, Jerrold B., et al. "Clinical Features and Management of Intoxication Due to Hallucinogenic Drugs." *Medical Toxicology and Adverse Drug Experience*, 4 (September–October 1989).

Lilly, John C. *The Center of the Cyclone*. New York: Julian Press, 1972.

Liska, Ken. The Pharmacist's Guide to the Most Misused and Abused Drugs in America. New York: Collier Books, 1988.

"LSD (Lysergic Acid Diethylamide)." *NIDA Capsules*. Rockville, Md.: NIDA, January 1995.

Lyttle, Thomas. "Misuse and Legend in the 'Toad Licking' Phenomenon." *International Journal of the Addictions*, 28 (May 1993).

Martin, Christopher S., Patrick R. Clifford, and Rook L. Clapper. "Patterns and Predictors of Simultaneous and Concurrent Use of Alcohol, Tobacco, Marijuana, and Hallucinogens in First-year College Students." *Journal of Substance Abuse*, 4 (1992).

Mitchell, S. Weir. "The Effects of Anhalonium Lewinii (The Mescal Button)." *Lancet*, 2 (1896).

Moseley, Bill. "Still Crazy After All These Years." *Psychology Today*, 28 (January–February 1995).

Natale, Michael, C. C. Dahlberg, and J. Jaffe. "The Effect of Psychotomimetics on Therapist-Patient Matching of Speech Rhythms." *Journal of Communication Disorders*, 12 (February 1979).

National Directory of Drug Abuse and Alcohol Treatment and Prevention Programs. Rockville, Md.: Substance Abuse and Mental Health Services Administration, 1992.

Nelson, Chad C., and Rodger L. Foltz, "Chromatographic and Mass Spectrometric Methods for Determination of Lysergic Acid Diethylamide (LSD) and Metabolites in Body Fluids." *Journal of Chromatography*, 580 (September 1992).

Osmond, Humphrey, "On Being Mad," in Bernard S. Aaronson and Humphrey Osmond (eds.). *Psychedelics: The Uses and Implications of Hallucinogenic Drugs.* Garden City, N.Y.: Anchor Books, 1970.

Peroutka, Stephens J. "Incidence of Recreational Use of 3,4-Methylenedioxymethamphetamine (MDMA, 'Ecstasy') on an Undergraduate Campus." *New England Journal of Medicine,* 317 (December 10, 1987).

Preliminary estimates from the 1993 National Household Survey on Drug Abuse: Advanced Report Number 7. Rockville, Md.: Substance Abuse and Mental Health Administration, (July 1994).

Robbins, Paul R., Roland H. Tanck, and Herman A. Meyersburg. "Psychological Factors in Smoking, Drinking, and Drug Experimentation." *Journal of Clinical Psychology,* 27 (October 1971).

Santisteban, Daniel A., and Jose Szapocznik. "Bridging Theory, Research, and Practice to More Successfully Engage Substance Abusing Youth and Their Families into Therapy." *Journal of Child and Adolescent Substance Abuse,* 3 (1994).

Scher, Mayonda, and Vernon Neppé. "Carbamazepine Adjunct for Nonresponsive Psychosis with Prior Hallucinogenic Abuse." *Journal of Nervous and Mental Disease,* 177 (December 1989).

Schwartz, Richard H. "LSD: Its Rise, Fall, and Renewed Popularity Among High School Students." Pediatric Clinics of North America. In press.

Schwartz, Richard H., George D. Comerci, and John E. Meeks. "LSD: Patterns of Use by Chemically Dependent Adolescents." *Journal of Pediatrics,* 111 (December 1987).

Schwartz, Richard H., and Deborah E. Smith. "Hallucinogenic Mushrooms." Clinical Pediatrics, 27 (February 1988).

Smart, Reginald G., and Dianne Jones. "Illicit LSD Users: Their Personality Characteristics and Psychopathology." *Journal of Abnormal Psychology,* 75 (June 1970).

Spoerke, David G., and Alan H. Hall. "Plants and Mushrooms of Abuse." *Emergency Medicine Clinics of North America*, 8 (August 1990). A History. Norman, Okla.: University of Oklahoma Press, 1987.

Stewart, Omer C. *Peyote Religion: A History.* Norman, Okla: University of Oklahoma Press, 1982.

Strassman, Rick J. "Human Hallucinogen Interactions with Drugs Affecting Serotonergic Neurotransmission." *Neuropsychopharmacology,* 7 (November 1992).

————. "Human Hallucinogenic Drug Research: Regulatory, Clinical and Scientific Issues," in Geraldine C. Lin and Richard A. Glennon (eds.), *Hallucinogens: An Update.* NIDA Research Monograph Series 146. Rockville, Md.: NIDA, 1994.

Szára, Stephen. "Are Hallucinogens Psychoheuristic?," in Geraldine C. Lin and Richard A. Glennon (eds.), *Hallucinogens: An Update.* NIDA Research Monograph Series 146. Rockville, Md.: 1994.

"*Tips for Teens About Hallucinogens.*" Rockville, Md.: Substance Abuse and Mental Health Services Administration. Undated.

Waltzer, Herbert. "Depersonalization and the Use of LSD: A Psychodynamic Study." *American Journal of Psychoanalysis,* 32 (1972).

Wasson, R. Gordon. "Seeking the Magic Mushroom." Life, (May 27, 1957).

Weil, Andrew, and Winifred Rosen. *From Chocolate to Morphine: Everything You Need to Know About Mind-Altering Drugs.* Boston: Houghton Mifflin, 1993.

Werner, Mark J. "Hallucinogens." Pediatrics in Review, 14 (December 1993).

Index

poisoning, 10, 84
post-hallucinogen perceptual
    disorder, 31
psilocin, 47
psilocybin, 47
psychedelic drugs, 6
psychoses, 6, 12, 14, 26, 63, 84–85

seeking help, 83–84, 86
self-mutilation, 14
serotonin, 32–33
shamans, 9, 37
shroomers, 45
single use risk, 30
Sixties rebellion, 56–57
space distortion, 41, 47
STP, 11
synesthesia, 26
synthetic versus plant origin, 6

tabernanthe Iboga, 7
talking down, 29, 83–84
time-distortiion, 27, 39
TMA, 11
toad-licking, 52
tolerance, 32, 43, 51, 75

V

violence, 14, 84
visual impairment, 33

W

Wasson, R. Gordon, 47, 48, 49
window panes, 23

Y

yagé, 7